INDUSTRY
AND INFANTRY
★

THE CIVIL WAR ★ IN WESTERN PENNSYLVANIA

INDUSTRY AND ★ INFANTRY

THE CIVIL WAR ★ IN WESTERN PENNSYLVANIA

Edited by Brian Butko and Nicholas P. Ciotola

Historical Society
of Western Pennsylvania

Published by HSWP
Senator John Heinz Pittsburgh Regional History Center
1212 Smallman Street
Pittsburgh, PA 15222
www.pghhistory.org

Printed in the United States of America

10 9 8 7 6 5 4 3 2 1

First Edition

Principal contents previously published in *Western Pennsylvania Historical Magazine*, a publication of the Historical Society of Western Pennsylvania.

Design by Kendra Power Design & Communication, Inc.

Front cover: top, and blue and red insets, from "Pittsburgh's Fort Pitt Foundry," *Harper's Weekly*, 23 August 1862 [HSWP Library & Archives]; bottom and yellow inset: Veteran Company B, 63rd Regiment Pennsylvania Volunteers, c. 1863 [HSWP Library & Archives]; green inset: Col. James Childs with officers of 4th Pennsylvania Cavalry, c. 1862 [Library of Congress].

Frontispiece: Col. James Childs with officers of 4th Pennsylvania Cavalry, c. 1862 [Library of Congress].

Back cover: The Duquesne Greys inside Allegheny Arsenal, Lawrenceville, 1870 [from *The Twenty-Eighth Division in the World War*, vol II, 1924, HSWP Library & Archives, Library collection]; flag of Company H, 62nd Pennsylvania Volunteers, the Saint Clair Guards [Captain Thomas Espy Post No. 153 of the Grand Army of the Republic, at the Andrew Carnegie Free Library, Carnegie, Pa.]; a stereoview card of Allegheny City Hall as it looked for the Pittsburgh Sanitary Fair [HSWP Library & Archives, stereo card collection].

Library of Congress Cataloging-in-Publication Data

Industry and infantry : the Civil War in western Pennsylvania / edited by Brian Butko and Nicholas P. Ciotola.– 1st American paperback ed.
    p. cm.
Includes bibliographical references and index.
    ISBN 0-936340-11-8
    1. Pennsylvania–History–Civil War, 1861-1865. 2. Pennsylvania–History–Civil War, 1861-1865–Social aspects. 3. United States–History–Civil War, 1861-1865–Social aspects. I. Butko, Brian. II. Ciotola, Nicholas P. III. Historical Society of Western Pennsylvania.
    E527.I53 2003
    973.7'09748–dc21

2003005637

CONTENTS

ACKNOWLEDGMENTS

Right: Civil War veterans of West Alexander, Pa., probably photographed by Lloyd Gibson, and **below**, the minie ball that started Andy Masich's life-long fascination with the war. — both Andrew Masich

A S A YOUTH, I DISCOVERED A CIVIL WAR "MINIE BALL" IN GRANDFATHER LLOYD Gibson's dusty attic. The Gibsons had settled in West Alexander, Pa. — a National Road "pike town" in Washington County — in the 1780s. I grew up hearing the exploits of West Alexander Civil War veterans.

Hooked on the lore of war, I read voraciously and even went so far as to convert my boyhood bedroom into a Civil War museum, complete with hundreds of bullets and cannon balls.

Years later, I was drawn back to Pittsburgh by the attraction of Western Pennsylvania's rich history. I immediately began exploring its Civil War history, and finding that much pioneering work had already been done, proposed the idea of compiling a volume of the best Civil War articles from *Western Pennsylvania Historical Magazine*. Brian Butko, editor of *Western Pennsylvania History*, and curator Nick Ciotola enthusiastically embraced the idea and are largely responsible for bringing this edited anthology to fruition.

The staff of the Senator John Heinz Pittsburgh Regional History Center deserves first mention for providing support and assistance. Senior Vice President Betty Arenth deserves praise for acknowledging the merits of the publication and identifying the often elusive funding needed for such a project. Other colleagues, chiefly David Halaas, Anne Madarasz, Barbara DeTemple, Rob DeOrio, Ann Fortescue, Steve Doell, Sharon Watson-Mauro, Douglas MacGregor, David Grinnell, Kerin Shellenbarger, Eli Paul, Lora Hershey, and Amanda Dunyak Gillen assisted us in varying degrees. In fact, all employees of the History Center, past and present, deserve recognition for helping in innumerable ways. It is our sincere hope that this book is not considered an achievement of individuals, but of the institution.

We extend special thanks to Bob Sandow, a doctoral candidate at Penn State University; Dana Shoaf, editor of *America's Civil War* magazine; and Gerard Patterson, author of *Debris of Battle: The Wounded at Gettysburg*, for taking the time to review, critique, and comment on the essays that appear in this volume. Their erudite suggestions were invaluable to the process by which formed our editorial commentary. William Blair and William Pencak, editors of *Making and Remaking Pennsylvania's Civil War*, and Art Fox, author of *Pittsburgh During the American Civil War, 1861–1865* also deserve mention, as does historian Michael G. Kraus, narrator of the video, "Civil War Minutes." The success of their recent publications greatly influenced our decision to compile another book on this topic. Kyle Weaver of Stackpole Books provided sound editorial advice and guidance as this project unfolded. Of course, the authors of the eight articles that comprise this volume must be acknowledged as well; it is their scholarship that was the most significant factor in making this book a reality.

A capable team of student interns and volunteers assisted with the tedious tasks of retyping, reformatting, proofreading, and fact-checking the articles, including Jennifer Randazzo, Steve Piper, Katie Farrer, Michael Schwille, Neal Hoage, and Greg Swiderski. Richard Christner, the compiler of the exhaustive bibliography of Civil War essays appearing in *WPHM*, immeasurably simplified the task of identifying the articles considered for republication.

ANDREW E. MASICH
President and Chief Executive Officer
Historical Society of Western Pennsylvania

FOREWORD

THERE ARE ESTIMATED TO BE MORE THAN 100,000 BOOKS AND ARTICLES published on the American Civil War. The question is often asked, "What more can be written about the war?" In the case of the Pittsburgh and Western Pennsylvania, the answer is "plenty." I initially became aware of this in the mid-1990s, when I embarked upon what would become my chosen field of historiography study.

During the four years of war, Pennsylvania supplied approximately 344,000 men for the Union Army and Navy. Nearly 26,000 of these came from Allegheny County, and tens of thousands more came from other Western Pennsylvania counties. Between 1861 – 1865, Pittsburgh-area camps of "rendezvous" served the western part of the state. Local craftsman, small workshops, and factory complexes under U.S. Government Ordnance Department contracts contributed to the Union cause. The Fort Pitt Foundry (in the present Strip District) alone produced over 2,300 pieces of heavy artillery, among them six 20-inch cannons, the largest ever forged in any U.S. foundry during the war.

Far from being a "backwater" city during the war, thousands of Union troops were supplied with munitions and equipment fabricated at the U.S. Allegheny Arsenal in Lawrenceville, while nearly a half-million soldiers passing though the city were fed by the city's aid societies. The U.S. Government Hospital (West Penn), then in Polish Hill, treated nearly 3,000 Union and Confederate soldiers. Almost a dozen of the Confederate troops lay at rest in Allegheny Cemetery. Fears of a Confederate attack against Pittsburgh in 1863 resulted in the construction of 37 earthen forts and redoubts on the city's hilltops. Confederate soldiers did finally arrive here, but as prisoners-of-war, incarcerated in Allegheny City's Western Penitentiary for several months in 1863 – 1864.

The history of Pittsburgh in the 1860s has long been overshadowed by the industrial era of big steel ushered in with the opening of Andrew Carnegie's Edgar Thompson steel works in Braddock in the 1870s. Aside from microfilmed newspapers, primary and secondary material of the Civil War era has been difficult to locate.

The following collection of articles explores many different facets of the war's impact on the region. All appeared decades ago in the society's journal, *Western Pennsylvania Historical Magazine*, forerunner to the present *Western Pennsylvania History* magazine. Long-time readers of the historical society's publications will recognize some of the eminently qualified historians authoring articles in this collective work. Having experienced the inconvenience in locating and copying some of these decades-old articles while conducting research for my new Civil War book, I can appreciate their renewed availability. Researchers reading my *Pittsburgh During the American Civil War* now have at their fingertips some of the complete articles that I employed and cited in my bibliography.

ARTHUR B. FOX

Author, *Pittsburgh During the American Civil War, 1860 - 1865*

INTRODUCTION

ROM THE INDUSTRIES THAT OUTFITTED THE UNION MILITARY WITH NAVAL VESSELS, cannons, ammunition, and medical supplies to the soldiers who filled the ranks of its massive volunteer infantry, Western Pennsylvania played an integral, though often overlooked, role in the northern war effort during the American Civil War. On home front and battlefront, Western Pennsylvanians rallied behind the cause of preserving the Union and participated in record numbers in both the defense of the commonwealth and the subjugation of the Southern insurrection. Upon receiving news of the Confederate attack at Fort Sumter, for example, thousands from the Pittsburgh region heeded President Abraham Lincoln's initial call for 90-day volunteers. Mustered into service at Camp Wilkins or one of Pittsburgh's other Civil War camps, many of these young men, and the officers who commanded them, remained in the military for the duration of the war, providing the manpower needed for the Union's eventual military success. Western Pennsylvania women, meanwhile, played an important behind-the-scenes support role exemplified by their work organizing the Pittsburgh Sanitary Fair of 1864, an event that raised thousands of dollars for the relief of sick and wounded Union soldiers. Pittsburgh industries, too, marked an important component of the Union war effort. The Fort Pitt Foundry, for instance, produced heavy ordnance and military accoutrements throughout the war years while Pittsburgh's shipbuilding firms built ironclad vessels for the Union Navy.

Despite these noteworthy contributions, the extant literature on the role of Western Pennsylvania in the American Civil War remains relatively unknown. In recent years, however, two publications have proven instrumental in bringing about newfound attention on this subject. Published by Penn State University, a national center for the study of Civil War history, *Making and Remaking Pennsylvania's Civil War* challenges the popularly held notion that the history of the Civil War in Pennsylvania revolves exclusively around the Battle of Gettysburg. Rather, editors William Blair and William Pencak argue that the Civil War impacted the commonwealth of Pennsylvania in a number of other important ways. Comprised of 10 well-written, thoroughly-researched essays, the volume examines manifold aspects of Pennsylvania's Civil War including the motivations of soldiers, gender and race issues during wartime, the impact of the war on Pennsylvania's civilians, and, of course, aspects of the Battle of Gettysburg. The publication sheds light on some aspects of Pittsburgh's Civil War history, particularly the life and legacy of noted abolitionist Charles Avery of Allegheny City (now Pittsburgh's North Side). This essay notwithstanding, the book focuses principally on events and personalities in the eastern and central portion of the commonwealth, a bias characteristic of many works addressing the history of Pennsylvania.

Arthur Fox's *Pittsburgh During the American Civil War, 1860 – 1865* marks an equally important contribution to the literature dealing with the impact of the War Between the States on communities in the region. Fox's book, unlike *Making and Remaking Pennsylvania's Civil War*, focuses exclusively on Western Pennsylvania, particularly on the city of Pittsburgh. Meticulously researched and encyclopedic in scope, the book amasses a wealth of information about Pittsburgh's Civil War camps, military industries, hospitals, prisons, subsistence agencies, and Grand Army of the Republic posts. Most noteworthy is the author's in-depth discussion of the Allegheny Arsenal and Fort Pitt Foundry, two operations that established the city as one of the leading suppliers of materiel for the Union military. Taken together, these books mark important contributions to the literature on this aspect of Pennsylvania history and have brought about a renewed interest in the subject among scholars, Civil War historians, and the general public.

Scholarship dealing with the Civil War in Western Pennsylvania, however, began long before the publication of the two aforementioned texts. The quarterly journal of the Historical Society of Western Pennsylvania has long been the leading publication venue for Western Pennsylvania-related Civil War writing. Between 1927 and the present, more than 60 articles dealing with the region's Civil War history have appeared in *Western Pennsylvania Historical Magazine* or its two later iterations, *Pittsburgh History* and now *Western Pennsylvania History*. Few aspects of Western Pennsylvania's Civil War history remain untouched in this little-known treasure trove of historical research. It is a valuable, if rarely used, resource for any student or scholar interested in the region's Civil War history.

Industry and Infantry: The Civil War in Western Pennsylvania brings back into circulation some of the most significant Civil War articles to appear in *Western Pennsylvania Historical Magazine* over the course of the 20th century. Considering the great number of quality essays from which to draw, the process of selecting the chapters that comprise this volume proved particularly difficult. Three factors governed the selection process: relevance to the topic at hand, quality of research and writing, and geographical representation across the region. Admittedly, many articles addressing compelling topics had to be omitted from this volume due to constraints of time and space. An article dealing with Pittsburgh African Americans in the Civil War was not selected for re-publication because the content of the essay dealt almost exclusively with the exploits and achievements of the 54th Massachusetts Volunteer Infantry Regiment, a subject documented at length in other publications and chronicled in the classic 1989 motion picture *Glory*. The somewhat condescending tone of the essay, reflecting the biases of the era in which it was written, as well as the lesser quality of research and writing, also influenced our decision to omit this article. However, it leaves the door open for researchers to more adequately explore the topic. Similarly, an essay dealing with the fear of invasion panic that seized Pittsburgh during the summer of 1863 was omitted from this volume since the subject had been tackled in depth elsewhere, most recently in a thorough, two-part article in the Fall and Winter 1998 issues of *Pittsburgh History*. We encourage readers interested in the many articles not selected for republication in this volume to consult the back issues available at the Historical Society's Library & Archives.

Written across the span of many decades, the articles comprising this book represent a wide variety of writing styles, mannerisms, and literary nuances. Some were originally presented orally and then reprinted verbatim in the journal, while others were written directly for publication in a formal, academic prose. We have opted to reprint the essay narratives as they originally appeared, with few additions or alterations. The editorial insertions that we have made, which appear in brackets, are meant to correct proven inaccuracies or provide the reader with information considered essential for understanding the content of each essay. We have also chosen to begin each chapter with a brief introductory statement that provides additional contextual material. Finally, we reformatted and standardized all of the endnotes, being sure to insert additional information about source material if it was not included in the original publication. These additions, we hope, have made the essays more readable and more reliable while maintaining the integrity of the original versions.

Overall, this compilation represents an important contribution to the literature on the Civil War in Western Pennsylvania. The articles span the duration of the war, beginning with the historic election of 1860 and ending with Pittsburgh in the postwar period. Individual essays cover numerous aspects of the war including the efforts of local communities to mobilize for war, the day-to-day experiences of soldiers and their commanders, pre- and postwar politics, military industries, and the impact of women on the home front. Taken collectively, they make an important statement about the overall role that Western Pennsylvania played in the War Between the States. Ideally, this volume will also stimulate a newfound appreciation of the Civil War in the region and serve as a catalyst for continued documentation of this significant aspect of Western Pennsylvania's past.

BRIAN BUTKO AND NICHOLAS P. CIOTOLA

Pittsburgh, Pennsylvania
January 2003

CHAPTER 1

WESTERN PENNSYLVANIA AND THE ELECTION OF 1860

BY JOSEPH P. WOLSTONCRAFT

Historians view the presidential election of 1860 as one of the most significant races in American history. The campaign pitted Abraham Lincoln and the fledgling Republican Party against three candidates — Stephen Douglas, representing northern Democrats; John C. Breckinridge, representing southern Democrats; and John Bell, the candidate of the Constitutional Unionists, an ad hoc party made up largely of ex-Whigs and remnants of the American Party, or Know-Nothings. In 1860, Pennsylvania citizens were engrossed not only in the well publicized presidential race, but in a significant gubernatorial election – one that elected Andrew Curtin as Pennsylvania's wartime governor. In this essay, Joseph P. Wolstoncraft explores the complicated political climate of Western Pennsylvania on eve of the American Civil War and the reasons why the region largely threw its support behind the Republican Party in the historic elections of 1860. This essay was originally read before the Historical Society of Western Pennsylvania on 31 May 1923 and appeared in the January 1923 issue of *Western Pennsylvania Historical Magazine*.

Left: Andrew G. Curtin, governor of Pennsylvania, 1861 to 1867. From *Lives of the Governors of Pennsylvania* by William C. Armor (1872). — HSWP Library & Archives, Library collection

P ENNSYLVANIA, PREVIOUS TO 1860, HAD BEEN A STRONG DEMOCRATIC state and had come under the sway of James Buchanan, who had controlled Pennsylvania politics in the years preceding. From the election of Andrew Jackson, in 1828, until the election of Abraham Lincoln, Pennsylvania, with one or two exceptions, had been mainly Democratic. But now, in 1860, had come a great political revolution, for instead of giving the Democrats a majority, as had been the case, Pennsylvania gave Andrew Curtin the surprising majority of 32,084,[1] and Lincoln a majority of 56,673 over the combined votes of his three competitors [Stephen Douglas, John C. Breckinridge, and John Bell].[2] This large a majority surprised even the Republicans themselves.[3] In this election, furthermore, the Democrats received such a setback that they have never recovered the strength and prominence that they enjoyed previously. Now, such a revolution must have had some strong cause back of it, and it is the purpose of this paper to discuss why and how this change came about.

It was early recognized that Pennsylvania was to be the battleground of the campaign. If Lincoln was to be elected, he had to have the support of all the northern states. Especial significance was attached to Pennsylvania since she was to elect a governor in October. As early as 1 November 1859, Lincoln wrote to W.E. Frazer, "It is certainly important to secure Pennsylvania for the Republicans in the next presidential contest,"[4] and throughout the ensuing campaign, this idea was stressed.[5]

The *Pittsburgh Daily Gazette* of 21 August 1860 said, "The great fight of November is to be settled in Pennsylvania by the preliminary fight in October. If we elect Curtin, ... the election of Lincoln will be settled; if we lose Curtin, ... the fight in November will be close and doubtful.[6] As Pennsylvania goes, so goes the Union."[7] The *Pittsburgh Post* said, "Circumstances point to the old Keystone, a State which must decide the pending Presidential contest."[8]

The campaign preliminaries in Pennsylvania started in January, when the friends of Simon Cameron started to mention him as a candidate for the Presidency. His name was rapidly taken up and great enthusiasm was manifested for him in the opposition press. The *Washington Reporter* said, "The union of the opposition forces so essential to success in the coming Presidential struggle could best be secured by the nomination of either Edward Bates, Cameron or William Dayton"[9] and the Republicans of Fayette[10] and Mercer Counties instructed their delegates to the State Convention to "support all measures calculated to secure the nomination of Simon Cameron at the Chicago Convention."[11] Lincoln himself was not adverse to supporting Cameron, if he was nominated, for he said, "If the Republicans of the great State of Pennsylvania shall present Mr. Cameron as their candidate for the Presidency, such an indorsement for his fitness for the place could scarcely be deemed insufficient."[12] At the State Convention, "The enthusiasm for Senator Cameron was unbounded, carrying all before it, and overshadowing the claims of all his distinguished competitors"[13] and by a vote of 127 to four, [14] the delegates to the Republican National Convention were "instructed to cast their votes for Honorable Simon Cameron while his name remained before that body."[15] Accordingly, Cameron's name was presented to the National Convention at Chicago, and on the first ballot he received forty-seven and one half votes out of the fifty-three cast by Pennsylvania. However, it was thoroughly understood that Pennsylvania's first vote was merely a "complimentary vote for a favored son"[16] and did not determine how she would vote in the remaining ballots. On the second and third ballots, Cameron's name having been withdrawn,[17] most of Pennsylvania's votes were thrown to Lincoln so that on the third and deciding ballot, Pennsylvania gave Lincoln fifty-two votes out of fifty-four cast.[18] The same evening her delegation brought on the platform a banner bearing the inscription, "Pennsylvania is good for 20,000 majority for the Peoples' candidate for President."[19]

Pennsylvania, and especially Cameron, had much to do with the nomination of Lincoln and particularly with the defeat of William H. Seward. The state, as has been said above, was debatable ground and it was admitted that if she was ignored in the nomination the Republican Party would have to do without her at the election.[20] It was the determined position of the doubtful states, and especially

Pennsylvania, which prevented the nomination of Seward for the delegates from these states said they could not carry their home states for Seward.[21] In Pennsylvania, Seward was opposed on account of his radical views in regard to slavery and also on account of his opposition to the American Party, to which most of the Republicans of the state had belonged.

The news of Lincoln's nomination was received in Allegheny County and the neighboring counties with "joyful and enthusiastic acclamation on the part of the Republicans."[22] In Pittsburgh, cannon were discharged from Boyd's Hill and flags were flung to the breeze.[23] In Washington, "A large and enthusiastic meeting convened in the Court House to ratify the nomination of Lincoln and Hannibal Hamlin" and although the notice of the meeting was short and there was a heavy rain, the courtroom was filled.[24] Cameron, the political boss of the state, "made an excellent speech … endorsing the nominations of Lincoln and Hamlin in a most cordial and emphatic manner."[25] Practically all the opposition journals in the state favored Lincoln and, on this point, the *Gazette* said, "There are at least 150 opposition journals in Pennsylvania, and of these, two, or at most three, support the Baltimore nominations," [26] the rest favoring Lincoln.

Meanwhile, the Democrats had held their convention at Charleston, South Carolina, which resulted in the withdrawal of the radical element of the South.[27] The Democrats of Western Pennsylvania were practically a unit in desiring Stephen Douglas, for we find the *Post* remarking, just before the delegates left for the second National Convention, "It is idle for the delegates from Western Pennsylvania, who are now about to go to the Democratic Convention at Baltimore, to pretend that they do not understand the wishes of the people whom they represent, in regard to the Presidential nomination. Too often and in too many ways the people have spoken out for Douglas to leave any doubt that he is their choice."[28] After the permanent split, the *Post* claimed that Douglas was the regular nominee of the National Democratic Party, saying, "The Senator from Illinois was nominated fairly and honorably, according to every Conventional rule and usage of the party,"[29] and "There is — there can be — but one candidate of the National Democratic organization, and that candidate is Stephen A. Douglas…. The agents of the people at the Baltimore convention nominated Mr. Douglas; from that day it was a closed question."[30]

The main issues of the campaign, it seems, were: one, the tariff; two, slavery in the territories; and three, sectionalism. The first of these, the tariff question, played an important role in the election. Pennsylvania at this time was just recovering from the Panic of 1857, which had crippled the industrial interests of the state to a large extent. As the tariff then in effect was a low Democratic tariff, it was decided that the remedy was a high protective tariff, which the "people considered essential to their prosperity."[31] The demand in this state for a protective tariff led to the introduction of a tariff plank in the Republican Platform of Chicago.[32] The Republicans, seeing their opportunity, took a strong stand on the matter of a high tariff,[33] saying that protection was "one of the cardinal purposes of the national government"[34] and "one of the cardinal doctrines in their creed."[35] They also cited Curtin as a lifelong advocate of protection.[36] The Democrats, realizing the importance of the tariff question, also came out strongly for a protective tariff,[37] although they were somewhat handicapped by the fact that the National Democracy was for free trade or a low tariff and also by the fact that the Panic of 1857 had occurred under a Democratic administration and tariff.[38] Both parties had tariff planks in their county and state platforms.[39]

Another important issue was that of extension of slavery. The Republican Party was fundamentally an anti-slavery party and as such received support in the other northern states. Although in Pennsylvania the tariff was a vital issue, especially in manufacturing districts such as Allegheny County, slavery was of some importance. But in their opposition to slavery, it must be remembered that the Republicans did not assume as radical a stand as did the Abolitionists. They were willing that slavery should remain in the slave states but they were opposed to its extension in the territories.[40] The two main arguments of the Republicans against slavery were the unconstitutionality of slavery and the effect of the spread of slavery upon free labor.

As to the unconstitutionality of slavery in the territories, the Republicans declared emphatically that the Constitution did not recognize slavery and called attention to the fact that the revolutionary fathers "excluded the words 'slave' and 'slavery' from the Constitution, that James Madison said he thought it wrong to admit into the Constitution the idea that there could be property in man," and that their "policy … was to make the national domain all free."[41] The Republican State Convention, in an Address to the People of Pennsylvania said, "That the dogma that the Constitution, of its own force, carries Slavery into all or any of the territories of the United States, is a new and dangerous political heresy, at variance with the explicit provisions of the instrument itself, with its contemporaneous exposition, and with legislative and judicial precedent, that it is revolutionary in its tendency, and subversive of the peace and harmony of the people."[42] The *Lincoln Herald*, quoted by the *Gazette*, said, "The Constitution of the United States does not establish or prohibit slavery. Slavery is an institution growing out of state laws and cannot exist beyond the limits of such state. The natural condition of all territories is freedom, and should be kept free."[43] The Republicans said further:

With the Constitutionally guaranteed rights of the Slave States, they have not and never will intermeddle.... Where slavery is under the Constitution they will never enter to disturb it or meddle with the existing relations of master and slave. But when the question of new states arise, when the virgin soil of broad land is to be subdivided into new confederacies, then the Republican Party claims to be heard in behalf of Freedom, and will not be slow to enter its solemn protest against the desecration of one other foot of free soil to the barbarous and anti-Christian institution of slavery. Hands off where slavery now exists under the Constitution ... but no more slave states.[44]

The other argument of the Republicans against the spread of slavery, namely, that of the effect upon free labor, had much more influence than the one just mentioned. The Democrats, especially those of the South, were working for the spread of slavery into the territories and, with the aid of the Dred Scott decision, for the spread of slavery into the free States. [In actuality, this was an accusation made by the Republicans. Democrats by and large did not advocate expansion of slavery as a party platform.] The Republicans made much of this fact to appeal to the working men of the manufacturing districts. The Republicans in 1854 had lost Pennsylvania on an anti-slavery platform, showing that the slavery issue was not very strong.[45] But now it was brought nearer home by showing the effect that slavery would have upon the laboring class of Western Pennsylvania. J.G. Blaine showed the importance of this issue very plainly when he said, "The moment the hostility to slave-labor in the territories became identified with protected labor in Pennsylvania, the Republican Party was inspired with new hopes, received indeed a new life."[46]

The *Gazette* made good use of statements expressed by Southern leaders and papers regarding slavery and the working class, such as: "We believe capital should own labor," from a speech made by Herschel V. Johnson, the running mate of Douglas; "The South now maintains that Slavery is right, natural and necessary, and does not depend upon difference of complexion. The laws of the Slave States justify the holding of white men in bondage," from the *Richmond Enquirer*; and "Slavery is the natural and normal condition of the laboring man, whether white or black.... Master and slave is a relation in society as necessary as that of parent and child, and the Northern States will yet have to introduce it. The theory of free government is a delusion," from the *Charleston Mercury*.[47]

The *Gazette* used these quotations with great effect. They showed the laborer the danger he would encounter in working in competition with slaves, and also showed him that in the end he would probably become a slave himself or, if not a slave, a "poor white." The *Gazette* remarked further, "It is remarkable that Southern Senators, in speaking of poor men and working men, invariably speak of them in opprobrious terms. Sen. Hammond called them 'the mudsills of human society;' Mr. Wigfall denounced them as 'criminals' and declared poverty to be a crime; and here comes Mr. Green who stigmatizes them as 'poor, infamous scoundrels' and 'lazzaroni.' There is no discrimination — no exception. Every man who is poor and compelled to work for a living is, in the eyes of these aristocrats, infamous and base from the very fact of being poor. And these men are Democrats — leaders in the Democratic Party — its advocates and oracles."[48] Edgar A. Cowan, in a speech in Pittsburgh on 26 September, said, "I am not asking you to liberate the slaves — I am no abolitionist; it is the poor white men we want to liberate, first."[49] Carl Schurz condensed the Republican stand as follows: "To man — his birthright; to Labor — freedom; to him that wants to Labor — work and independence; to him that works — his dues."[50]

The Republicans made so much use of this argument that they were enabled to say, towards the end of the campaign, "The real and true issue between the two great parties which underlies all the struggles and strife, is, whether the power of government shall be exerted to protect free white labor or black slave labor. Divested of the shams and deceptions, that is the whole contest when narrowed down to its practical point."[51] Now, with this argument of protected white labor and the argument of protection to the industries, we can see that the Republicans would have a great hold upon the people of the Pittsburgh district.

The Douglas Democrats in Western Pennsylvania took a middle stand on the slavery question, advocating "popular sovereignty" and "non-intervention by Congress." The Democratic State Convention states their stand very well in the following resolutions:

> Resolved, that we deprecate the continued agitation of the slavery question in Congress and among the people in the different sections of the Union, believing, as we do, that it tends to weaken the bondage of our common union — to excite animosities and create heart-burnings between the members of the same great family, and can accomplish no possible good. Resolved, that we continue firm in the opinion that Congress has no power to legislate on the subject of slavery in the States, nor would it be expedient for Congress to establish it in any territory, or to exclude it therefrom. Resolved, that the question of the right of the citizen to hold his slaves in the Territories of the United States is a judicial, and not a legislative question, and its decision is committed exclusively to the courts.[52]

Herschel V. Johnson, the candidate for the vice presidency, devoted the whole of his speech in Pittsburgh to the question of slavery and non-intervention by Congress.[53]

The *Post* says, "The Democrats, at least in the North, are not slavery propagandists. Where slavery exists, they are willing to defend it from all interference of outside aggressions. They are willing that the people of new territories and new states shall decide for themselves whether the institution shall exist within their borders or not."[54] The Democrats also accused the Republicans of being Abolitionists, saying that, "The great object of every Democrat in the present campaign should be to defeat the Abolition Candidate Lincoln,"[55] and the *Washington Review* condemned Lincoln several times for being an Abolitionist.[56]

The third great issue of the campaign, which was used mainly by the Democrats, was that of sectionalism. The Republicans, of course, were strictly a northern party, there being no Republicans in the South. The *Post* says, "The prominent candidates are Lincoln and Douglas. The one represents Sectionalism — the other Nationalism,"[57] and a little later sums up the situation thus, "The Republicans are trying to elect a President for the North. The Bolters are trying to elect a President for the South. The National Democracy are trying to elect a President for the whole Union."[58] The Republicans denied the charge of sectionalism saying that they "indignantly hurl back in the teeth of its utterers the foul imputation of 'sectionalism' and 'one ideaism' so flippantly imputed to them by the subsidized press of the Democracy, and boldly assert their just claims to be considered the broad comprehensive national party of the Country."[59] The *Post* also professed to see a connection between Republican Sectionalism and Southern threats of disunion, for it said, "The very foundation of the Republican party of the North is a mad fanaticism which has brought the country to the verge of destruction. It is the principles of Republicanism openly avowed by its leaders as the issue of the campaign, which have aroused in the South those fierce disunion sentiments.... Northern fanaticism has bred Southern Disunionism."[60]

A variation of the sectionalism argument used by the Democrats was that the aggression of the Republicans was leading to the severance of the commercial relations between the North and the South. The Democratic County Convention at Pittsburgh approved the following resolution:

> Resolved, that we ... disapprove of all attempts to alienate the South from the North, by interference with Southern institutions, because such interference leads to a breaking up of the international trade between the citizens of the several states, a trade which has been a source of vast profit to Pennsylvania and because an interruption of that trade must seriously interfere with the market for the great staples of our commerce ... that give employment to thousands, that confer wealth and prosperity upon our cities, and secure a market for the produce of the farmer.[61]

The *Post* said, prior to the meeting of the Convention:

> Already the business men of the North begin to feel the influence of the present political estrangement from the South. The natural effect of such aggression as the North is making upon the South is to destroy the business relations between the two sections ... The southern people are quietly but firmly making their arrangements to cut off their business intercourse with the North. They are forming among themselves non-intercourse compacts and are directing their trade as far as possible away from the northern manufacturers and business men.[62]

Although the Democrats were of one mind in their purpose of defeating the Abolitionist candidate Lincoln, they were nevertheless engaged in a family quarrel. Buchanan, the Democratic political boss, supported the Southern Democrats both before and after the Democratic Conventions, thinking that the road to power lay through the South.[63] The majority of the Democrats of the State, however, favored Douglas. Buchanan brought to bear all the power possible to secure the state for John C. Breckinridge, but failed. The main struggle between the two factions was in regard to the Democratic State electors. The electors had been named at the State convention at Reading before the national party had split. The question now arose: Whom shall the electors vote for in case the Democrats carried Pennsylvania, Douglas or Breckinridge?

It was clearly seen that, if the Democrats expected to carry the state in both elections, they must present a united front[64] and, accordingly, all efforts were made to do this. At a meeting of the State Central Committee held in Philadelphia early in July, "Mr. Welsh's compromise plan to have but one electoral ticket, unpledged to either, but to cast its vote, if elected, for the Democratic candidate most likely to be successful, was ... adopted."[65] This plan was denounced by the people and the press as an "infamous proposition."[66] The *Post* said that it was willing to support a single electoral ticket but maintained that the decision as to whom the electors should vote for should be left to the people and not to the State Committee or to any future contingencies which the people cannot control as they wish.[67] Richard Vaux, the head of the Electoral Ticket also refused to approve of the compromise.[68] The Douglas faction, at a convention at Harrisburg, likewise opposed this attempt at coalition and further resolved to demand that the State Committee should rescind this action and come out for Douglas, at their Cresson meeting of 9 August 1860.[69]

At the Cresson meeting, the State Committee "resolved on a Fusion Ticket, headed by the names Douglas and Breckinridge, the vote of the electors to go to the one who has the highest number of votes in the State."[70] The *Post* approved of the plan, saying, "The first object now is success, and to do this, we must have a united and harmonious organization, as against the common enemy.... We shall sustain the action of the Committee at Cresson, because it is the only way we see to preserve the integrity of the State organization under present circumstances,"[71] and "We are for it, because it will elect Henry D. Foster, Governor, and preserve our good old Democratic party a unit."[72] Some of the more radical Douglas men, however, objected to this compromise and "kicked out of the traces."[73] The Douglas State Executive Committee, on 15 August, resolved to place a "clear Douglas electoral ticket" in the field.[74] The *Post* "as the friend of Mr. Douglas, and an ardent desirer of his success" condemned the movement, and said further, "No true friend of Douglas can, with any consistency, favor this Harrisburg movement. It is, in fact, a Bolter's ticket."[75] This ticket, however, was withdrawn on 18 October[76] enabling the Democrats to present a united front in the presidential election.

In the October election for Governor, Curtin, the Republican candidate, carried the State with a vote of 262,396 to 230,312 for Foster. The result in Allegheny and the surrounding counties was as follows:[77]

County	Curtin	Foster
Allegheny	15,879	9,190
Westmoreland	4,830	5,276
Butler	3,526	2,548
Beaver	2,682	1,717
Washington	4,768	4,206

In the Presidential election in November, Lincoln carried the state with a vote of 268,030 as compared with 178,871 for the Fusion Ticket, 16,677 for the Douglas straight ticket and 12,809 for the Union Party. The result by counties was as follows:[78]

County	Lincoln	Fusion	Douglas	Bell
Allegheny	16,725	6,725	523	570
Westmoreland	4,887	4,796	13	13
Butler	3,640	2,332	13	22
Beaver	2,824	1,620	4	58
Washington	4,724	3,975	8	91

An examination of these figures reveals that in the industrial centers, such as Allegheny County, where the main issue was tariff and protected free labor, the Republican majority was large, whereas in the agricultural counties, where the issue was the extension of slavery, the vote was nearly even. It would appear that the result of the October election influenced somewhat the November election in as much as we find that in almost every case, the Republican vote was larger and the Democratic correspondingly smaller. This is possibly due to the natural desire of those who had no decided opinions, to be on the winning side. Westmoreland County, which went Democratic in the state election by a majority of about 450, owing no doubt to the fact that it was Foster's home county, gave the Republicans a majority of 90 votes in the Presidential election.

In conclusion, I wish to emphasize these two facts: first, that the success of the Republicans in Western Pennsylvania was due largely to their strong stand on the question of tariff, protected free labor and non-extension of slavery, and in part to the split in the Democratic Party; second, that the success of the Republicans in Pennsylvania contributed in a marked degree to their success throughout the Nation. [The importance of the Democratic Party split in the election of Abraham Lincoln is subject to debate. Even if all of the Lincoln opposition is taken in sum, Lincoln would have still likely emerged victorious in the election]. ★

CHAPTER 2

NEW CASTLE IN 1860-61: A COMMUNITY RESPONSE TO A WAR CRISIS

BY BINGHAM DUNCAN

The Confederate bombardment of Fort Sumter in April 1861 precipitated immediate and profound reactions from communities throughout Western Pennsylvania. To some, news of the outbreak of war was shocking and unexpected. To others, conditioned by frequent coverage in the region's newspapers, the incident in Charleston Harbor proved an inevitable result of the growing sectional crisis. In this essay, Bingham Duncan explores the collective reaction of one Western Pennsylvania community, New Castle, to the outbreak of the American Civil War. Beginning with a discussion of the pre-war economy in New Castle and the community's perception of the growing antagonism between north and south, the author provides a community-centered case study that can be used to draw larger conclusions as to the region's overall response to war. This essay was originally read at the Twelfth Annual History Conference of the University of Pittsburgh, 26 April 1941, and was published in the December 1941 issue of *Western Pennsylvania Historical Magazine*.

Left: The only known image of New Castle's Civil War troops leaving town appeared in *Souvenir Program, New Castle Sesqui-Centennial, 1798-1948*. The view is looking east on Washington Street at Mercer, 21 April 1861. — HSWP Library & Archives, Library collection

H ISTORIANS AND OTHER WRITERS HAVE FREQUENTLY DESCRIBED THE IMPACT of the Civil War on northern and southern economic and social institutions. There are, however, relatively few studies of the effects of the war crisis upon local communities such as towns and counties.

This article does not pretend to be a full study of the impact of the Civil War upon New Castle, Pennsylvania, but rather seeks to point out some of the more outstanding elements of New Castle's response to the approach of this conflict. Because of the magnitude of their effects, their unexpectedness, and the rapidity of development, the events between the election of Abraham Lincoln and the First Battle of Bull Run produced in New Castle such a reorientation of business life, political activity, and psychological outlook as to constitute a local crisis. The limits of the crisis may, therefore, be defined as beginning with the recognition that war was possible and continuing until the secession of the Border States, in June 1861, provided a background for the acceptance of a new routine of war effort.

The north central part of Lawrence County, of which New Castle was the leading town, was at this time in the midst of a transition from an agricultural to an industrial economy. The change began with the erection of the Aetna Iron Works in 1839. During the next 20 years a number of iron manufacturing establishments were set up in New Castle, and by 1837 iron manufacturing was the principal business of the town. The furnaces, rolling mills, and nail factories were supplied with ore and limestone from nearby hills and could turn out products varying from three-penny nails to railroad iron. All together, iron manufactures in New Castle were valued at $154,000 in 1860; the nearest commodities in value were flour and meal, valued at $140,000.

This industrial development was temporarily arrested by a serious depression between 1859 and 1863. One of the two most important of the New Castle iron-works, the Orizaba, which manufactured some 7,500 tons of iron and nails per year during the 1850s, was idle from 1859 to 1863. Machinery rusted; men whose only income had come from the mills and factories of the Orizaba since its establishment in 1845 were without means of supporting themselves; and many who could find no other employment were forced to move out of New Castle during 1860 and 1861. A purchaser was not found for the furnaces, keg factory and dozens of nail machines, which together were called the Orizaba Iron Works, until 1863. In that year the Beaver Valley Railroad, connecting New Castle with the road from Erie to Pittsburgh, was finished, allowing coal to come into New Castle other than by wagon and canal (frequently frozen during the winter months) and giving new life to the iron manu-facturing industry. The depressed condition of industry in the county was further accentuated by the dissolution of the Cosala Iron Company, with two-thirds the productive capacity of the Orizaba, in 1857, and by the abandonment of the charcoal blast furnace 10 miles away, at New Wilmington, in 1860. Neither of these appear to have been revived during the war years.

No important efforts to restore New Castle's industrial prosperity were made during the years from the beginning of the depression in 1857 to the establishment of the railroad in 1863. This lack of effort was due partly to the presence of oil in the region nearby; as each new well or rumor of a well came in, the hope was expressed that New Castle would soon become the center of a great oil industry. It is perhaps too much to say that New Castle was a stagnant town during the months of the war crisis, but its rate of growth was slow (the decade 1850 to 1860 showed an increase from 1,614 persons to 1,882), and there was no industrial or other economic devel-opment to give its citizens a sense of pride in an expanding community.

It will be noted, therefore, that the months between Lincoln's election and the secession of the Border States were contained within a period of depression for New Castle, as they were for a large part of the Shenango-Beaver Valley and for much of the country.

Neither the election of November 1860, nor the secession talk that developed in the gulf states during October and November drew from New Castle a response comparable to the gravity of the crisis into which the country was being drawn. Republicans were prepared to do what was necessary to eliminate slavery or at least to confine it in those places where it then existed. Democrats showed considerable doubt as to the wisdom of electing a sectional candidate to the presidency, particularly in view of possible southern disaffection. However, the party's leaders in New Castle expressed the opinion, as early as 17 November, that secession would amount to treason. Even then the problem was considered largely an academic one as no articulate group seemed to want or expect war. As the secession movement grew through November and early December the reaction of New Castle people, as far as can be ascertained, was one of surprise and curiosity rather than of resentment and excitement.

During the first fortnight of the month of December the activities of the Lower South began to be discussed around the "cracker barrels" and on street corners. Unfortunately we do not have transcripts of any of these discussions; such comments as appeared in local papers suggested that they were not heated as late as 22 December, although the paper of that date carried an account of the proceedings of the South Carolina secession convention.

Despite the paucity of extant documentary evidence, it cannot be doubted that New Castle was conditioned for the coming crisis by a wide acceptance of anti-secessionist feeling and widespread suspicion of southern democracy. Expressions of such feeling in January and February are plentiful and suggest that feelings were expressed verbally during the early weeks of the crisis rather than in writing. One interesting bit of evidence of the breadth and depth of this attitude is shown in the action of the editor of the *Lawrence Journal*. In 1849, in the first year of its publication under the editorship of J.M. Kuester, this paper avowed Jeffersonian and Jacksonian principles, opposed the "peculiar institution" of the South, and claimed the distinction of printing all the news. At this time there was a well-organized Whig party in Lawrence County. The Whigs continued to grow, becoming Republican in time to support Lincoln. The *Journal*, however, remained Democratic; during the campaign of 1860, Kuester supported Stephen Douglas and Herschel Johnson and the straight Democratic ticket, urging his readers to do likewise. [In the 1860 election, the Democratic Party was split into two wings reflecting regional loyalty: Northern Democrats, with the exception of Buchanan supporters, tended to support the Stephen Douglas and Herschel Johnson ticket for president and vice president; Southern Democrats backed John C. Breckinridge and Joseph Lane].

Immediately after the election Kuester expressed the opinion that Lincoln's election might cause hard feelings in some quarters but indicated that all real Americans should abide by the decision of the electorate. Early in December he printed a rather sharp criticism of the president-elect; this proved to be his last important objection to Republicanism during the months of the crisis. Within less than a month, in the issue of 5 January 1861, the editor of the *Journal* was forced to abandon his Democratic tenets and to begin using the slogan "A Local Family Newspaper — Independent on All Subjects." This action he explained as follows:

> For a number of years we have been publishing a political journal, and as papers belonging to certain faiths cannot find admittance in every family we have assumed this new position to obviate the difficulty, as we wish the Journal to find a place in every family. The Journal [is] generally acknowledged [to be] the best paper in the county but on account of politics was discarded by many.... As we are now independent we ask the people to support us in our new undertaking.

Of the other papers in New Castle, one, the *Gazette*, was edited by a W.H. Shaw who supported the war to the extent of leaving his position in 1862 to take a more active part in the struggle. The other, the *Courant*, had been the abolitionist *American Freeman* until purchased by a Mr. Durban in 1857.

During January, the third month of the war crisis, increasing attention was paid in New Castle to the progress of the secession movement, the supplying of the garrisons at Pensacola and Charleston, and the military preparations in Georgia. Speeches of secessionists were described in local papers under such headings as "The Progress of Treason" and "The Mobocratic Spirit of William Yancey." Still, New Castle lagged behind the eastern part of the state in its activities. Union meetings, such as were held in Philadelphia before Christmas, did not gather in the New Castle area until 22 January. The first such meeting occurred in the Westminster Chapel at New Wilmington. Those who attended considered the crisis a grave one, their purpose in assembling as peaceful, and Andrew Jackson and his phrase "the Union must be preserved" as immortal. They opposed compromises that might tend to nationalize slavery or allow it to be extended to the territories, and condemned those who incited slaves to rebel.

In New Castle the anti-compromise forces were gaining strength though there was still a strong element that was ready to compromise on the basis of "no extension of slavery." New Castle's first Union meeting was held on George Washington's birthday. But so great was the intensity of concentration on the issue at hand that the "Father of His Country" was not mentioned in the resolutions condemning secession, concession, and compromise. These resolutions, stronger in their opposition to compromise than those made at New Wilmington, were sent to Washington in the name of the Republicans of Lawrence County.

With the Union meeting over, and their attitudes having been given formal expression, the literate public in New Castle, minds now made up, turned toward Washington and watched the new president for indications of the precise steps to be taken in the critical weeks of March and April. During these weeks emphasis was laid on a reexamination of the political principles of the Constitution, the American system of government, presidential powers and other political-legal aspects of the question at issue. The full text of Douglas' plea for compromise by constitutional amendment was printed in the 23 March issue of the *Lawrence Journal*; an editorial comparing the United States' and Confederate States' constitutions appeared the following week; a series of lectures on political science, signed "Junius," began in the 6 April issue in order to "break the shackles from the minds and bodies of men." These were dropped after Fort Sumter.

At the same time the nearest outside paper, the Republican *Mercer County Dispatch*, seemed not opposed, as late as 27 March, to the idea of a broken union. The editor thought that the idea of two confederacies was widely held in Washington by leading Republicans including two or three cabinet members. He added:

> I can say, furthermore, that the executive acts bearing upon the Southern question will be largely influenced by a belief in the one probable contingency of a separation, and a desire to make it a peaceable one. While it is deemed due to the honor and dignity of the government, both at home and abroad, to vindicate its authority in the seceded States, and while blows will be struck if necessary, it will be only to redeem the credit of the federal power, and not to permanently maintain its authority over an unwilling people.

The editor seemed, at this time, to expect that a national convention would be called to settle all grievances and that Virginia would remain in the Union. His chief worry was that the low Confederate tariff would lure commerce away from northern ports.

On receipt of the news of the firing at Fort Sumter, New Castle, already morally prepared, responded immediately and decisively. Considerable surprise was shown but the community was well prepared psychologically for the outbreak of war. The firing at Sumter occurred on Friday, 12 April 1861. The news arrived in New Castle that night, and on Saturday morning, Dr. Daniel Leasure began enrolling names of those who wished to fill out the Lawrence Guards, a military unit organized shortly after the Mexican War. Lincoln issued his call for volunteers on Monday; all business activity in New Castle ceased for the remainder of the week; and the Lawrence Guards were filled and parading by the end of the week. Phrases such as "the memory of Washington," "the Flag of Our Country," "an appeal has been made to the God of Battles," " righteous cause," and "the American Eagle fears not to brave the mad rebellion" appeared in editorials and letters to the editors of local papers. Anti-Confederate propaganda, lacking before Sumter, appeared in stories showing how the slave states had adopted many of the practices they had formerly condemned, such as tariffs and export duties. Reviewing the "Effects of Southern Repudiation," on 8 June, the editor of the *Lawrence Journal* wrote:

> Since this rebellion has broken out these States have again commenced their old game of repudiating their honest debts due by their citizens to the citizens of the loyal States and the amount of indebtedness thus repudiated amounts to millions of dollars. The morality of this course is shocking to every honest man. The moral sense of Christendom is shocked by this want of commercial honor and common honesty. Whatever may be the result of this war and its result is not doubtful the credit of these States is gone forever.

Quips suggesting that Heaven, Purgatory, and Hades were represented respectively by the northern states, border states, and seceded states were passed around. By the end of the week, ladies were on the streets collecting money with which to buy material for flags to contain 34 stars each; a meeting was called to raise "substantial aid" for the dependents of volunteers and for outfitting the Lawrence Guards.

In short, New Castle was preparing to carry on a segment of the war, using its own resources and drawing upon its own manpower. The first contingent of the Lawrence Guards, fully organized and officered and partially equipped, left for Pittsburgh at eight o'clock Sunday morning, six days after Lincoln's call, after a send-off party had offered prayers, made speeches, and played martial music to speed them on their way.

On Monday, 22 April, New Castle sent a second detachment of the Lawrence Guards, 33 strong. Business was still at a standstill. For the protection of the county in the absence of the natural defenders who were volunteering in large numbers, the veterans of the War of 1812, calling themselves the Silver Grays, formed, with some 40 to 50 boys who were too young to volunteer, a home guard; an early move was to burn Jeff Davis in effigy. [Organized throughout southwestern Pennsylvania, home guards were militia units consisting of older men and boys charged with protecting their respective communities from enemy raids and invasion]. At the same time other towns in the county were organizing home guards as well as volunteer companies; New Castle formed the Rifle Guards and the Zouaves in addition to the Lawrence Guards.

Institutionalization of New Castle's response to the war crisis was begun at a mass meeting held in the public square on 24 April. This meeting made itself a convention and after the usual prayer, speech, and martial music, proceeded to adopt a number of resolutions relating to the crisis. Had the program planned at this meeting been carried out it might well have been considered the initiation of

a war program rather than a move in the crisis, but the plans were superseded
by others after the nation, state, and county realized that the political crisis was to
become a major war and to last for years instead of months. The resolutions adopted
at the mass meeting called for drill for all able-bodied men; the collection of equipment such as bandages and blankets for all who were drilled; gifts of grain, money,
and clothing to support the fighting men; and readiness for instant service in
defense of Lawrence County.

In this connection it is interesting to note that nowhere in the discussions
during the critical weeks is there any suggestion that offensive efforts are to be
made. Phrases used in letters to the editors of local papers, in comments from other
places printed in local papers, and in editorial comment in no case assumed an
attack on another people. Rather, men wrote of defending the flag, Constitution, and
laws of the United States; of the flag having been attacked; and of the honor of the
country needing defenders. During these weeks there was little disposition to con-
sider the constitutional aspects of the secession movements any further. Papers
demanded that their readers be "men or mice," and "for or against" the rebels; men
assured each other that the cause for which they were preparing to fight was a
"holy and a just cause"; and that the opposition was guilty of fraud, treachery, wrong,
and despotism. In Mercer, the editor of the *Dispatch* wrote that the prayers of
thousands followed all Mercer troops and that their memories would be cherished
as having offered themselves a sacrifice at their country's call, whether they fell
in battle or succumbed to disease.

While these attitudes were being expressed, during later April and through
May, other and more practical aspects of the war crisis began to become evident.
Horses were needed by the growing army; under a quota system Lawrence County
farmers from the New Castle area sold 16, from "a large number" brought in, at
an average price of $125 each; a Mr. A. Cubbison, three weeks after Sumter, had
secured a stock of drums, drumsticks and fifes from New York to sell to the con-
stantly growing number of New Castle volunteers; farmers planted more seed in
anticipation of good prices for food crops.

On the other hand, the already serious problem of industrial unemployment
was further complicated by the necessity of providing relief for wives and children
of volunteers, many of whom were left without means of support when their
husbands and fathers went off to war. The problem had been foreseen when men
were encouraged early in April to join the Lawrence Guards, and leading townsmen
had called a meeting to provide dependents of volunteers with "substantial aid."
Collections for this purpose were taken up, but although the sum raised proved
insufficient, no further attempts were made until late May, after the state had acted

to establish local boards of relief and to define the procedure to be followed by those needing relief. During the spring of 1861, New Castle women whose husbands were in the army and who had no children received from 75 cents to a dollar and a quarter a week. Family groups that included from one to five children were allowed from one to three dollars per week depending on the circumstances as seen by the local relief board. These sums were sufficient to provide sustenance except in some cases where rents of 50 cents to a dollar per week had to be paid out of the allotted amounts. The relief question was not settled satisfactorily during the crisis months.

From this brief account of New Castle's history it can be seen that the average inhabitant was affected in many ways by the events that transpired between Lincoln's election and the Battle of Bull Run. Sympathy for the problems faced by the southern states was replaced almost immediately after the firing at Sumter by agreement that secession constituted treason and that the rebel leaders were morally depraved; the patriotism of those who sympathized was considered some-what questionable. This condition was exemplified by the *Lawrence Journal's* switch to "independence" from "Jeffersonian and Jacksonian democracy" because "papers belonging to certain faiths cannot find admittance to every family." The *Journal's* "independence" further emphasized the awakened interest of the community in a question of such proportions and significance that its own problems became insig-nificant by comparison. Rumors of oil wells still evoked interest in the late spring of 1861, but such news was no longer as important as it had been earlier.

The idea of war was kept ever before the populace by women and men too young or too old to fight. The women formed committees for the purpose of making flags, bandages, and other articles considered necessary for the defense of the country. Boys and veterans of the War of 1812 organized a home guard which helped to unify opinion in New Castle. Drives to collect gifts of money, blankets, grain, and clothing were made by these and other groups. Finally, New Castle's contribution to the armed forces made important differences in the life of the town. The early enlistment of two companies of volunteers from a population of 2,000 persons immediately and directly affected a fifth of New Castle's population. In those cases where the departure of a volunteer meant the absence of a son, perhaps no hardship was experienced by other members of the family. But in many instances the volunteer had a wife, and frequently children; such cases involved community relief and social disorganization. On the other hand the departure of from 60 to 80 able-bodied males had some salutary effects on a community that had suffered under conditions of unemployment for from two to three years preceding the crisis months. A further helpful element in the matter of employment was the increased business activity brought on by the sale of army supplies, including food.

By the beginning of the summer of 1861, then, New Castle had experienced a number of changes in the life considered normal during the preceding fall. The day-to-day responses to events of the crisis months were merging into a unified program of war effort involving a shift in employment, new business activity, the administration of relief, and a greatly broadened outlook on national problems. ★

DO YOU LOVE YOUR COUNTRY?

IF SO, RALLY FOR HER DEFENSE!

YOUNG MEN,

Your Country demands your service. Come forward, then, with willing hands and brave hearts, to crush out treason!

A FINE OPPORTUNITY

Is now offered to persons desiring to enlist for three years or during the war, by the

DUQUESNE ZOUAVES!

Now in camp, near Pittsburgh, who require a few more good active men to fill up their ranks to the complement of 101. This Company is attached to the

INDEPENDENT SKIRMISHERS

ACCEPTED IN

COL. HIRAM HULTZ'S REGIMENT.

Persons wishing to join will please call immediately at

No. 61 Wood Street,

UNDER LAFAYETTE HALL, PITTSBURGH.

Or _____

D. M. ARMOR, Capt.

W. S. Haven, print, Pittsburgh

CHAPTER 3

CAMP WILKINS, MILITARY POST, 1861

BY JOSEPH A. BORKOWSKI

One of Western Pennsylvania's most noteworthy contributions to the American Civil War was providing thousands of soldiers to fill the ranks of the Union Army. In April 1861, widespread enlistments in Pittsburgh, New Castle, Washington, Erie, and other Western Pennsylvania communities precipitated a pressing concern — the need to establish a central location to assemble, train, drill, and equip the new recruits for service in the Union Army. Throughout the course of the war, Pittsburgh was home to a number of Civil War camps, among them Camp Howe, Camp Montgomery, and Camp Copeland. In this essay, Joseph Borkowski provides an overview of the formation and function of Camp Wilkins, Pittsburgh's first location for quartering the region's Civil War soldiers. The camp was located in what is today Pittsburgh's Strip District, in a part that is mostly warehouses and rail yards. Although only in existence for several months, Camp Wilkins played an important role in the process by which the region's young enlistees underwent their transition from citizens to soldiers. This essay first appeared in the September 1962 issue of *Western Pennsylvania Historical Magazine.*

Left: The camp mentioned in this handbill was Camp Wilkins, now part of Pittsburgh's Strip District. From *Under the Maltese Cross*, edited by Charles F. McKenna (1910). — HSWP Library & Archives, Library collection

WHEN PRESIDENT LINCOLN ON 15 APRIL 1861 ISSUED HIS FIRST CALL for 75,000 militia "to repossess the forts, places and property which had been taken away from the Union," the response of the people of the city of Pittsburgh was electric.[1] The city's already organized military companies answered to such an extent that there were more than enough to meet the initial quota assigned to the Pittsburgh area. Enthusiasm to defend the Union was widespread throughout the area. Even before the formal call for recruitment was under way, volunteer companies from outlying regions of western Pennsylvania started to converge on Pittsburgh.[2]

Many companies on arrival were without means of support. Not being officially enrolled, they could not draw upon military funds. To accommodate incoming recruits, a committee "for quartering troops and furnishing providence" was organized under the chairmanship of Samuel McKelvy on 27 April 1861 at the Board of Trade rooms, 78 Fourth Avenue, "to make arrangements of different volunteer companies who are ready to enter the service of the government."[3]

Headed by Judge William Wilkins,[4] the Citizens' Committee of Defense, of which McKelvy's committee was a part, appealed to Governor Andrew G. Curtin of Pennsylvania to permit the military companies "now here to form a camp under the direction of the military department."[5] Governor Curtin's first reply, however, stated that he was in no official position to give any orders until he was fully authorized to do so by the Legislature, which was scheduled to convene the following Tuesday.[6]

In the meantime the Citizens' Committee sought accommodations for the volunteers at the fair grounds[7] which were located on the south side of Penn Avenue between the present Twenty-ninth and Thirty-second Streets and extended to the Pennsylvania Railroad in Lawrenceville. Mayor George Wilson of Pittsburgh wasted no time in contacting Governor Curtin. He asked the governor formally to establish a military camp in the city in order to take care of the incoming concentration of volunteers and particularly to secure payments for accommodations and provisions.

On Saturday evening 27 April, Mayor Wilson and Mr. McKelvy left for Harrisburg on behalf of the Committee on Troops and Provisions following receipt of this telegram dated 27 April 1861:[8]

> MAYOR WILSON: On further consideration I have concluded to form a military camp at Pittsburgh. You will please have the companies marched into the camp immediately. I will name a commanding officer today. /s/ A.G. Curtin.

The news was received with unbounded enthusiasm, especially by the Citizens' Committee, which was entrusted with providing facilities and provisions to the men. The *Pittsburgh Gazette* had editorialized earlier that "it would furnish an opportunity for testing the realities of camp life and acquiring more proficiency in military discipline." The writer went on to take the liberty of naming the fair grounds area "Camp Wilkins and let it be the camp of the West."[9]

The local Committee on Troops immediately issued the following order:[10]

> Pittsburgh, April 27, 1861
> The respective companies who have reported to the Committee as ready to render their services to the government will assemble at the Fair Grounds on Monday morning April 29th at 10 o'clock to be formed in camp by the commanding officer.
>
> S. McKelvy, Chairman

A telegram the next day, however, changed the situation and consequently created much confusion and consternation among the local military units.[11] It read as follows:

> John W. Riddle: An officer appointed by the Governor will arrive at Pittsburgh tomorrow to organize Camp Wilkins. Allow no troops to go into Camp until he arrives.
>
> George Wilson
> Samuel McKelvy
> By order of the Governor

The newly appointed officer was Colonel Phaon Jarrett, and upon his arrival on 29 April, he immediately set out to make the fair grounds acceptable quarters for the incoming troops, thereby gaining much praise for his promptness and efforts.[12] However, the local committee became indignant when it was announced by Colonel Jarrett on 1 May 1861 that only six companies from Allegheny County would be accepted.[13] Twenty-eight additional companies had been alerted by their respective leaders and were ready to report to Camp Wilkins, and the Citizens' Committee felt it was an undue burden to feed and clothe the uncalled volunteers. A special committee headed by ex-Governor William F. Johnston[14] and Thomas M. Howe[15] was formed to seek arrangements for those who were recruited and not called. Disgruntled, many recruited companies voted to disband and returned home.

The hectic activities and agitations surrounding Camp Wilkins did not deter Colonel Jarrett from organizing the camp into a respectable military establishment. As of 3 May 1861,[16] Camp Wilkins contained 16 companies (about 1,200 volunteers) including 10 companies from Erie under command of Colonel John W. McLane[17] and Lieutenant Colonel Benjamin Grant. The recruits slept four abreast in the cattle stalls, using straw for bedding and knapsacks for pillows.

The following regulations and training orders were put into effect by Colonel Jarrett:

ORDER NUMBER 1

First: Accepted troops arriving at Camp will be escorted to their respective quarters by assistant Quartermaster.

Second: As soon as troops are admitted in the camp, a guard will be placed at the gate to prevent persons from entering the grounds who are not connected with the camp.

Third: At 5 o'clock A.M. reveille will beat, the companies form in their respective streets and the roll will be called.

Fourth: From 5 1/2 to 6 1/2 A.M. Company drill.

Fifth: Breakfast at 7 o'clock; Guard mounting at 8 A.M.

Sixth: Between 9 A.M. and 12 M – The captains will devote their time principally to instructing the respective commands in the Schools of Soldier and Company.

Seventh: Dinner at 1 P.M.

Eighth: Between hours of 3 and 5 P.M. the captain will instruct the companies as instructed in No. 6

Ninth: Between drills the Captains will detail men for Police Duty. Particular attention to this order is enjoined.

Tenth: Supper at 6 1/2 P.M.

Eleventh: Tattoo at 9 1/2 P.M. Roll called.

Twelfth: At 10 P.M. Taps, when the lights will be put out, except in the officer's quarters and no loud talking or disorder of any kind allowed.[18]

The Commissary was in the charge of Major Henry A. Weaver,[19] who was credited with being a very energetic and enterprising procurement officer and who was purchaser of rations for the camp. Those consisted of salt beef, bread, crackers, coffee and sugar, which he was able to get in abundance. Dr. Franklin Irish[20] received the appointment of Surgeon to Camp Wilkins. Later he served with the Pennsylvania Seventy-seventh Infantry.

One of the first public requests made by Colonel Jarrett was for a camp flag.[21] Although he had tried to purchase one, none was available at any price, and he referred the matter to a local women's patriotic committee headed by Miss Lizzie Johnston.

On Sunday 3 June 1861 the formal flag presentation from the committee was made in a manner befitting the occasion. The ceremony took place at four o'clock, and the flag was presented to Colonel Jarrett by former Governor Johnston. The crowd was estimated by the newspapers to be 8,000, not counting those "on the hillside in the rear which was also covered with spectators."[22]

On Saturday 4 May 1861 Governor Curtin paid a formal visit to Camp Wilkins on his way to Harrisburg following a conference at Cleveland[23] with the governors of New York, Ohio, Indiana, and Illinois. At the time of the governor's visit, 24 companies were in the Camp Wilkins area.[24]

On 9 June, Colonel Jarrett received his orders to return to his regiment, the Eleventh, stationed at Camp Wayne, West Chester, Pennsylvania, and Colonel McLane was put in command of Camp Wilkins.[25]

Colonel McLane lost no time in issuing his first order forming the companies and regiments into two battalions. The First Battalion under command of Colonel L.W. Smith, Lieutenant Colonel C.F. Johnson, and Major Robert Anderson consisted of the Pittsburgh Rifles, Chartiers Valley Guards, City Guards Company B, Meadville Volunteers, Iron City Guards, Garibaldi Guards and Allegheny Rangers. The Second Battalion included the Anderson Cadets, Fayette Guards, Armstrong Rifles, Duncan Guards, Jefferson Guards, Clarion Union Guardsmen, McKeesport Union Guards, and Jefferson Riflemen and was commanded by Colonel George S. Hays, Lieutenant Colonel S.D. Oliphant and Major John W. Duncan.[26]

Despite the unbounded enthusiasm on the part of the male populace to enlist as volunteers to fight for the preservation of the Union, the Pennsylvania State Legislature was slow to make provision for Camp Wilkins. Consequently many companies were without uniforms, arms, ammunition, and even shoes. Some of the companies, such as the Anderson Infantry,[27] provided entertainment to raise funds for uniforms and other military needs.

Many local citizens and congregations became sponsors and benefactors. For instance, friends provided uniforms for the crack outfit of the Garibaldi Guards, who were well trained and disciplined but without any military dress. They were purchased through Messrs. J. & J. Vogel on Liberty Street at $8 per suit.[28] Dinners were prepared and served by local women's societies of Pittsburgh and various church organizations which adopted different military regiments. For instance, "the Ladies of the Liberty Methodist Episcopal Church on Saturday evening presented the Erie Regiment at Camp Wilkins with 500 pies which were distributed at a rate of fifty to each company." Also a public appeal had to be made for shoes, "as there are 50 to 60 men who were barefooted."[29]

In a few days the people of Pittsburgh and Allegheny County began to bring loads of provisions, blankets, stockings, underclothes — in short, everything that was calculated to add to the comfort and gratification of the regiments. For these kindnesses a strong feeling of friendship grew between the men of the regiment and the local citizens.[30]

In fairness to Governor Curtin, it can be said that, despite his best efforts, there was little he could do to alleviate the existing chaos in Camp Wilkins since legislative action was necessary. Until such action was taken, all he could offer was consolation and hope to those local military units. The following letter, dated 18 May 1861, was sent from "a committee of gentlemen" who wished to obtain more definite "information in reference to securing the acceptance of the numerous volunteer companies now organized in this vicinity":[31]

To His Excellency A.G. Curtin, Governor
Sir:

The undersigned, in connection with Captains Smith, Jackson and Snodgrass (now absent at Camp Scott), came home today as a Committee (at the request) of Col. McLean [McLane] at Camp Wilkins to ascertain from you the prospects of the Companies which we have the honor to Command; and as you will leave for Chambersburg before we can have a satisfactory interview, we beg leave to ask the following questions, viz: What Companies and what number of companies will you be likely to muster into the service of the United States, in the State of Pennsylvania, from Allegheny County? Is it the intention of the Commander in Chief to remove Camp Wilkins from the present situation? We have heard, with regret, rumors to this effect, and desire to urge upon Your Excellency the propriety of continuing to hold this, in our opinion, very eligible situation for a camp.

Would it not be in your power to take at least two regiments from Allegheny County, as they could be very promptly furnished, of well disciplined and well behaved troops?

At what time may the Companies selected expect to be armed and equipped?

We remain with great regard your very humble servants,

Geo. S. Hays, Captain Anderson Cadets

John W. Duncan, Captain Duncan Guards

The Governor, in his reply on the same day to the Committee, indicated that the number of companies from Allegheny County had been designated in official order as eight. He pointed out that they were to be used for the service of the state and that he had no authority to call for any more troops for the national government. "As to precise location of such Camp, I will be advised by Major General McCall who will in a few days make the necessary examination for that purpose." The Governor, in closing, reminded the Committee that it would be a long struggle and therefore cautioned them to be patient lest their spirits might become dampened.

After a time unrest grew among the local people about the location of the camp. It appears a fact that there were a number of valid reasons advanced by the press for removal of Camp Wilkins to a more suitable site. The papers pointed out that the Fair Grounds were too small to drill the 2,000 troops; that the proximity of the camp to the city had a demoralizing effect; that it was impossible to enforce proper discipline while the facilities for reaching the city were easy and available; that drunken brawls and fierce assaults were not infrequent among the volunteers, and that the area was unsanitary.[32]

Later that month General George A. McCall recommended removing Camp Wilkins to Hulton Station on the line of the Allegheny Valley Railroad, a little west of Hulton Station on lands belonging to Edward Grier. Influencing his decision was the fact that "the men will have every facility for bathing in the pure waters of the Allegheny."[33] He also thought that the training grounds would be more suited to military demands than those of Camp Wilkins.[34] The new military facility was named Camp Wright after John A. Wright, Governor Curtin's Military Aide and Consultant.

One of the first military units to be moved from Camp Wilkins to Camp Wright was the Erie Regiment under the command of Colonel McLane.[35] However, the opening of Camp Wright did not diminish the military activities at Camp Wilkins,[36] and after all, by 18 June 1861, nine companies were at the latter. As of 2 August 1861, Camp Wilkins took on a Federal status as indicated by the following letter to the Honorable Thomas M. Howe,[37] Chairman of the Committee for Subsistence of Soldiers:[38]

War Department August 1st, 1861

I am instructed to direct you to receive and muster into service at Pittsburgh in squads of 50 or more volunteers for three years service. These volunteers when mustered in, will be sent you to Camp Wilkins and be there subsisted by the Government with a supervision of yourself and officers.

I am Colonel your obedient servant.

Geo. D. Recoles, Assistant Adjutant General

This letter was also addressed to the commanding officer of the Third Cavalry, Lieutenant Colonel Emory, who was recruiting here.

Of special interest in this particular advertisement which appeared under the Military Notices:[39]

The Company of the undersigned having been accepted in the Kentucky Cavalry Regiment Colonel W.H. Young now in Washington, will leave to join that Regiment as soon as the Company is full. Twenty men are wanted to fill it. Pay commenced as soon as the men are enrolled. Apply to the undersigned at Camp Wilkins.

S.B.M. Young, Captain.

The months of August and September were the busiest in Camp Wilkins' existence,[40] and some of Western Pennsylvania's best outfits were going there. Among those bivouacking at Camp Wilkins at this time was the Dunlap's Creek Cavalry raised in Fayette County and commanded by Captain J.B. Davidson, First Lieutenant David Gilmore, and Second Lieutenant W. Brown. The Company was sworn into United States service by Lieutenant Hutchings of Colonel Emory's Third Mounted Regiment. Another body of well-trained troops numbering 670 men awaiting call was under command of Colonel Daniel A. Leasure.

However, the most spectacular as well as best known outfit of its day was Colonel Amos A. McKnight's Regiment, "The Wildcat," which within its organization included the following companies:[41] Mahoning Rifles commanded by Captain John Hastings from Punxsutawney, Jefferson County; Ringgold Artillery, Captain John A. Frease, Ringgold, Jefferson County; Brookville Rifles, Captain John Dowling, Brookville, Jefferson County; Washington Guards, Captain Artemus H. Tracy from Jefferson County; Union Guards, Captain James D. Kirk from Indiana and Jefferson Counties; Perry Rifles, Captain Hovey, Clarion County; Limetown Guards, Captain C.A. Craig, Greenville, Clarion County; Jackson Blues, Susquehanna River, Clearfield County.

Others that were ordered to report included the Company from Sewickley Township, Westmoreland County, Captain Mungo M. Dick; Simpson Light Infantry, Captain Alexander Hay; Lawrence Grays, Lieutenant James L. Banks; and also six companies totaling 540 men under command of Lieutenant Colonel Scott Carter.

On 4 September 1861, a Fire Company of Volunteers from McKeesport under charge of Captain J. Whighan also reported at Camp Wilkins ready for active duty.

Colonel Alexander Schimmelfennig's[42] Regiment of Philadelphia, later to be known as the Pennsylvania 74th Regiment, mustered into service 14 September 1861 and was rated as the best trained and disciplined. Colonel George S. Hays, M.D., of Allegheny County, during the month of September departed from Camp Wilkins with 500 men to join the forces of General George McClellan. Colonel Hiram Hultz was in command of four companies. Also reporting at Camp Wilkins were the Agnew Guards, named after Judge Daniel Agnew of Beaver Falls, who were slated to join up with Colonel Wilson's Regiment.[43]

As of 27 September 1861, Colonel James A. Elkin of United States Quarter-master Department was named the commander of Camp Wilkins,[44] while Colonel Schimmelfennig and Colonel Alexander Hays were in command of Camp Wilkins at various periods. During the month of October 1861 the following commanders and their troops were recorded in the Camp Wilkins area and were forming units of General James S. Negley's[45] Brigade: Colonel Frederick S. Stumbaugh[46] of Chambersburg, Pennsylvania, 77th Pennsylvania Volunteer Infantry; Colonel Henry A. Hambright of Lancaster, 79th Pennsylvania Regiment; Colonel William Sirwell,[47] 78th Pennsylvania Regiment; and Captain H.L. Vanolove of Lancaster, Cavalry Company Body Guard.

It was at this time that Secretary of War Simon Cameron on his tours paid an official call to Camp Wilkins and made an inspection of its facilities and 3,000 ready to serve militia and, according to contemporary accounts, "was duly and favorably impressed with camp's general appearance."[48]

The use of Camp Wilkins as a rendezvous for incoming troops began to wane as Secretary of the Commonwealth Eli Slifer called upon all commanders of companies to report immediately to the headquarters at Harrisburg that means of transportation might be provided for them.[49] Governor Curtin immediately followed with another order that all recruiting be stopped as Pennsylvania quotas had been met.[50]

With the need of trained troops on the battlefields and particularly in face of the Confederate advances and Union casualties, there was a mass movement of all available manpower from Camp Wilkins.[51] By 31 December 1861, Camp Wilkins and Camp Wright were no longer mentioned in the local news accounts. In fact, General Negley's bodyguard from Camp Wilkins consisting of 50 men and 100 horses from Kentucky were the last troops to be mentioned in local newspapers. When General Negley's Brigade left, there were apparently no other troops stationed at Camp Wilkins.[52] ★

CHAPTER 4

GENERAL JAMES SCOTT NEGLEY

BY ALFRED P. JAMES

During the American Civil War, Western Pennsylvania produced a number of regiment-, brigade-, and division-level officers who distinguished themselves on the field of battle. Colonel Strong Vincent, a native of Erie, was mortally wounded while leading the brigade that defended the extreme left of the Union Army of the Potomac at the Battle of Gettysburg. Born in Franklin in 1819, General Alexander Hays fought with distinction in the Seven Days Battles, commanded the division that helped to defeat Pickett's Charge at Gettysburg, and was killed in action at the Battle of the Wilderness. General John White Geary of Mount Pleasant, Westmoreland County, led a division under William Tecumseh Sherman in the Atlanta campaign and the March to the Sea, and later used his military career to become a two-term governor of Pennsylvania. In this essay, Alfred P. James provides a compelling overview of the life of yet another distinguished Western Pennsylvania officer, General James Scott Negley of Pittsburgh, including his war-time successes and his October 1863 removal from command, of which he was later exonerated. This essay first appeared in the April 1931 issue of *Western Pennsylvania Historical Magazine*.

Left: This portrait is signed, "To Cousin Rebecca Baum — my affectionate regard, Jas. S. Negley. Camp Washington, Sept. 12, 1860." — HSWP Library & Archives, GPC

T HE SUBJECT OF THIS SKETCH WAS OF SWISS GERMAN ANCESTRY. ORIGINALLY the family name was spelled Nagèli, and in Switzerland it has furnished more than one person of high distinction. A member of this Swiss family migrated to eastern Pennsylvania in the second quarter of the 18th century. His son, Alexander Negley, later moved westward, first to the neighborhood of Ligonier, Pennsylvania, and later, in 1778, to what is now the Highland Park section of Pittsburgh. Alexander Negley, the pioneer, is thus the founder of the Negley family of Pittsburgh history.

Of his numerous children, Jacob Negley was the grandfather of James Scott Negley. By marriage with a Winebiddle heiress, and by purchases, Jacob Negley added to his inherited landholdings until he was in possession of approximately 3,000 acres of land, then farm and pasture land, but now a populous part of Pittsburgh. Of the children of Jacob Negley, an elder son, Jacob Negley Jr., was the father of James Scott Negley; while a younger son, George G. Negley, long a prominent figure in that section of the region, was the father of several children still living in the neighborhood; and Sarah Jane Negley became the wife of Judge Thomas Mellon and the ancestress of the well-known Mellon family of Pittsburgh.[1]

James Scott Negley, son of Jacob Negley, Jr., and Mary Ann Scott Negley, was born in what is now East Liberty, Pittsburgh, Pennsylvania, on 22 December 1826.[2] His parents having died while he was yet a child, Negley was reared in the home of the Baum family,[3] one of whose members, Mrs. Kate Baum Shillito, survived until 7 October 1930, when she passed away at the advanced age of 85 years.[4]

At local public schools, this young scion of the Negley family secured the elementary and secondary education necessary for college entrance. For collegiate studies he entered the Western University of Pennsylvania,[5] the institution now known as the University of Pittsburgh.

At a very young age the future general appears to have become interested in militia service, and it is said that he joined the Duquesne Greys while only a college youth.[6] With the outbreak of hostilities with Mexico in the early summer of 1846, this company as a part of the First Pennsylvania Regiment was called into service.[7] Young Negley enrolled on 8 December 1846 and was mustered into service on 16 December 1846.[8] He is said to have served through the remainder of the war, participating in the battles of Cerro Gordo, La Porta, Las Vergas, and Puebla.[9]

On 1 June 1848, he was promoted to the rank of sergeant.[10] According to the *Pittsburgh Morning Post*, 18 July 1848, "J.S. Negley returned in good health." The young sergeant, not yet 22 years old, received his discharge from military service on 25 July 1848.[11]

On his return to civilian life, James Scott Negley, having now reached his majority and with the larger part of his life before him, engaged for a time in manufacturing pursuits.[12] But he soon left this field of activity and took up farming and horticulture, attaining a reputation as one of the most skilled horticulturists in the whole country.[13] From 1856 to 1861 he is annually listed in the Pittsburgh directories as "horticulturist."[14]

But the young farmer and horticulturist evidently retained his interest in military life and his touch with the local militia. Even before the outbreak of the Civil War he seems to have risen to the rank of brigadier general, in connection with the Eighteenth Division of the Pennsylvania Militia.[15] It seems to have been well understood in the winter of 1860-61 that his services were at the disposal of the state of Pennsylvania.[16] The natural result was that on 13 April 1861, the day after the firing on Fort Sumter, Brigadier General Negley received a telegraphic dispatch from Governor Curtin requesting his immediate attendance at Harrisburg.[17] Leaving that afternoon, Saturday,[18] he returned to Pittsburgh on Monday night.[19] Governor Andrew Curtin had put him in command of military affairs in the district and made him responsible for raising, equipping, and forwarding troops from this area.[20] According to the local newspapers, the promptness and energy displayed by General Negley in getting his command into service met widespread local approval.[21] Within 10 days, characterized by great and successful activity, he had accomplished the work assigned him. On 24 April 1861, he and the regiments which he had gotten ready were called away to Harrisburg and the eastern part of the state.[22] Here General Negley's troops became a part of the force acting under the direction of Major General Robert Patterson.

"On the twenty-ninth of April, General Negley issued his first General Order, assuming command of the 12th and 13th Regiments."[23] Moved to Lancaster, Pennsylvania, he was placed in command at Camp Johnston.[24] As late as 11 May 1861, his command lacked the necessary equipment for field service.[25]

Early in June, a circular of General Patterson, directing army movements, instructed General Negley to "move by rail as rapidly as possible and be established on the Hagerstown and Williamsport turnpike in Western Maryland."[26] On 17 June 1861, General Negley was ordered to advance to Williamsport,[27] but three days later he received an order commanding him to veer to the right and march to Sharpsburg.[28] While on this station, in the very first weeks of his service in the field, General Negley showed an uncanny ability to learn what the enemy were doing,[29] a feature which characterized his entire career in the Civil War.

At early dawn of 2 July 1861, General Patterson crossed the Potomac River with all the forces under his command.[30] General Negley's brigade evidently reached Martinsburg, Virginia, during the course of the day.[31] Here he remained for more than a week, for in a council at this place on 9 July 1861, General Negley, with other subordinates of General Patterson, advised a move to Charlestown, Harper's Ferry and Shepherdstown with the purpose of outflanking General Joseph E. Johnston in command of the Confederate forces in the Shenandoah Valley.[32] With his brigade, General Negley also took part in the skirmishes and futile maneuvers of General Patterson during the military operations of the next two weeks. But his troops were three months' volunteers whose term of service had expired, and most of them marched back to Harrisburg, where late in July they were disbanded.[33]

General Negley, it seems, returned to Pittsburgh early in August and began to raise new companies of volunteer infantry.[34] On 28 August 1861, he received authorization from the War Department to raise and organize two regiments of infantry for three years or the length of time of the war.[35] By the middle of October he had evidently succeeded in raising an entire brigade. A message from Louisville, Kentucky, on 16 October 1861, sent by Simon Cameron, Secretary of War, asking for reinforcements at that point,[36] was promptly followed by orders to General Negley to move his command at once to General William T. Sherman at Louisville.[37] Governor Curtin in person received Negley's brigade and presented the standards to them on the afternoon of 17 October 1861, and reported he found the regiments full, the men fully equipped and in excellent condition.[38] In five days, the brigade, 2,800 strong,[39] reached their destination by water transportation.[40] It was immediately sent to the camp on Nolin River, Kentucky, where it became a part of the forces under Brigadier-General Alexander M. McCook, operating against the Confederate line in the southern part of that state.[41]

At this time the brigade of General Negley consisted of the 77th, 78th, and 79th Pennsylvania regiments and two batteries,[42] a body of volunteer troops drawn mainly from Western Pennsylvania. At the end of November, by order of General Buell, a reorganization of his forces was made. General Negley's old Fourth Brigade was broken up. He was assigned to the new Seventh Brigade, composed of the 38th Indiana, 78th Pennsylvania, 79th Pennsylvania, and First Wisconsin regiments,[43] the beginning of a process which eventually was to leave General Negley with few if any Pennsylvania troops under his command.

For nearly four months, General Negley was stationed in southern Kentucky.[44] Then came the collapse of the Confederate front with the capture of Fort Henry and Fort Donelson in the middle of February 1862. Though specific references are lacking, it is evident that General Negley took part in the general advance of Buell's troops at this time. Late in March, his brigade reached Franklin, Tennessee,[45] and he was in command in Maury County, Tennessee, early in April.[46] In the absence of any record of his participation in the Battle of Shiloh or Pittsburg Landing, one week later, it is evident that General Negley's brigade remained in the reserves in occupation of central Tennessee during that famous conflict. For more than a month, General Negley seems to have remained in the vicinity of Columbia, Maury County, Tennessee.[47]

When in May 1862, General Buell began to move southward and eastward up the Tennessee River into northern Alabama, General Negley's brigade was pushed forward in the movement.[48] By his forced marches and quick strokes in this campaign in the middle of May, General Negley won high praise for himself and his command.[49]

In the first week of June, General Negley was in command of a raid which, beginning on the first of the month, plunged eastward from Fayetteville, Tennessee.[50] Surprising and scattering the intervening Confederate troops, he advanced to the neighborhood of Chattanooga, the strategic point in Confederate territory and, on 7 and 8 June, actually bombarded the city from across the Tennessee River.[51] The capture of Chattanooga, which would have been a major stroke in the war, was threatened; but General Negley's forces were inadequate to hold the city if captured. His position was too extended and adequate support was not available, so he was withdrawn by his superiors with the sanction of General Buell.[52]

From the records of the summer of 1862, it appears that General Negley, like

General Sherman, had a severe attitude toward the hostile civilian population of the South. An accusation of pillage and robbery of the civilian population was made against his troops in connection with the expedition in June against Chattanooga.[53] According to his own contemporary correspondence, General Negley instituted "most vigorous and determined measures against non-combatant secessionists" in his neighborhood.[54] The activities of guerillas against his forces in Maury County, Tennessee, probably caused this harsh attitude.[55]

In the middle of August 1862, a sudden change came over military affairs in Tennessee. General Braxton Bragg had initiated his remarkable campaign from Tupelo, Mississippi, via Chattanooga, against Tennessee and Kentucky. More than seven months of comparative inactivity on this front had doubtless led to some laxity among the Union forces. In the confusion in August, General Buell directed a complaint to General Negley for lack of adequate guards at important bridges and the absence of officers from his command.[56] When, however, General Bragg advanced into central Tennessee, orders from General Buell bade General Negley to fall back rapidly upon Nashville.[57] A concentration of all the forces under the command of General Buell was made, with Nashville as the point of concentration.

But Bragg slipped away through Tennessee toward Kentucky and it was necessary for General Buell to move rapidly to Louisville, Kentucky to prevent the capture of that strategic point. On his departure, he left General Negley in command at Nashville. General Buell's order to General George B. Thomas on 13 September 1862, instructed him to "leave the siege artillery and most of the cavalry with Negley."[58] These orders also said, "Post Negley at the defensible works and positions and at the capital and bridge and direct him to have twenty days rations at each for its garrison. He must defend his position to the last extremity." And having assumed command on 14 September 1862,[59] General Negley did defend his position to the last extremity. The vigor of his procedure was such as to arouse the antagonism of Andrew Johnson, the war governor of Tennessee, and cause him to request General Negley's removal from command.[60] But the important post was held against strong Confederate attempts to capture it in the absence of General Buell's main army.

Early in October, General Negley in a dashing raid against La Vergne, 15 miles east of Nashville, broke up a concentration there of Confederate forces gathering under Generals S.R. Anderson and Bedford Forrest and Governor Isham Green Harris for assault on Nashville.[61] In the middle of the month he was able to make a favorable report to General Buell.[62] Nevertheless General Negley's situation in an exposed and threatened position seems to have caused alarm.[63]

General Negley seems to have been fully equal to the responsibilities placed upon him. When early in November attacks were made upon the fortifications of Nashville, they were sharply repulsed.[64] In the language of an observer, General Negley "did everything that occurred to him as a vigilant officer to do.... The city was thereby held until the arrival of this army."[65] It seems safe to say that this particular service of holding Nashville in the autumn of 1862, was one of the most important of General Negley's military career.

During December the Union army at Nashville, now under General William S. Rosecrans, who had succeeded General Buell, found itself almost face to face with the Confederate army of Bragg, who had returned via Chattanooga and approached as close to Nashville as Murfreesboro on Stones River. On the severe Union defeat at Fredericksburg, Virginia, 12 December 1862, strong pressure was brought to bear upon General Rosecrans to restore the lost prestige by a vigorous campaign against the Confederate army of General Bragg. This Rosecrans proceeded to do during the Christmas week of 1862. One of the bloodiest encounters of the entire war was the result. In this encounter, General Negley commanded the troops in the center of the Union line. By heroic service on 30 December 1862, he prevented the line from being shattered and broken.[66] On the following day he was compelled to give away in orderly retreat.[67] On New Year's Day there was quiet along the battle front, but on 2 January 1863, the Confederates decided to fall back to Shelbyville and General Negley took part in a general advance.[68] The campaign ended with the retirement of General Bragg's army and the occupation of the immediate region by Union troops.

In a letter to President Lincoln, 24 February 1863, General Rosecrans recommended that seven of his brigadier generals, among them General Negley, be raised to the rank of major general.[69] Probably in response to this recommendation, there appears in the abstract from returns of the Department of the Cumberland ... for the month of March 1863, the item, "Second Division, Maj. Gen. James S. Negley."[70]

It seems that for more than five months, General Negley's Second Division of the Fourteenth Army Corps remained in the neighborhood of Murfreesboro.[71] But Rosecrans was planning an advance against Bragg whose forces had been depleted by troops sent to take part in the Vicksburg campaign. On 8 June 1863, Rosecrans consulted his subordinates about the wisdom of an aggressive move against Bragg's army.[72] General Negley advised against such an advance, unless all the forces could be thrown forward and cooperation secured from General Ambrose E. Burnside in command of Union troops in eastern Tennessee.[73]

In the military operations of July, August, and September, by which General Rosecrans outflanked General Bragg's positions and forced him back from Tullahoma through Chattanooga into Georgia, General Negley and his division played an important role. In the second week of September, while advancing in mountainous territory, his division was attacked by an overwhelming force and he was compelled to fall back temporarily.[74] The enterprise was becoming more difficult and dangerous and General Rosecrans began a hurried concentration of his badly scattered forces.

In the famous battle of Chickamauga, 20 September 1863, General Negley again found himself near the center of the line of battle. His division was stationed on the extreme left of the right wing of General Rosecrans' army. The battle began on the Union left wing. Some of General Negley's brigades were proceeding to the aid of the badly pressed Union left wing, when the Confederates found a hole in the line on the Union right wing, poured through, broke up the organization of the opposition and swept the larger part of Rosecrans' right wing back toward Missionary Ridge. General Negley with considerable artillery and a few disordered infantry regiments was caught in the milling crowd and pushed back to Rossville Gap. But so also were Generals Rosecrans, Alexander McCook, Thomas L. Crittendon, and Philip H. Sheridan.

Criticism accompanies failure and disaster. Some fellow officers sharply criticized General Negley,[75] and General Rosecrans evidently listened to the accusations. He was in none too good a position himself and he probably was searching for scapegoats among his subordinates. C.A. Dana, on 27 September 1863, notified Secretary of War Edwin Stanton that Rosecrans would proceed against Negley.[76] On 4 October 1863, Dana reported to Stanton that both he and Rosecrans thought Negley should be shot, and that he would be relieved of his troops,[77] a report the tenor of which was repeated on 17 October 1863.[78]

General Negley was relieved of his command, issuing his farewell address to his division on 10 October 1863.[79] In reporting the matter to the War Department, General Rosecrans said that General Negley left the battlefield "without orders."[80] He added, "The general has always been an active and efficient commander ... but an impression that he left the field on Sunday without orders or necessity having made its way through this army" he had been given a leave of absence of 30 days.[81] General Negley, quite properly, made a complaint to Secretary Edwin M. Stanton of the War Department.[82]

On the expiration of his leave of absence, he appears to have reported for duty in his old command, for C.A. Dana, on 18 November 1863, sent a message to Secretary Stanton, saying, "General Negley having reported to Thomas for duty from Nashville, Thomas replied that he could not give him a command until a court had cleared him from charges of cowardice and desertion at Chickamauga."[83] In another dispatch four days later,[84] Dana reported to Stanton, "Negley replied to

Thomas' suggestion that he should demand court of inquiry on imputations of cowardice and desertion, that he had fully satisfied you these charges were erroneous, and you had thereupon ordered him back to this department,"[85] and according to this dispatch, "Thomas then ordered him to remain in Nashville till further orders." But General Ulysses S. Grant one month later was even less considerate and courteous than General Thomas had been. In Special Orders No. 26, from Nashville, Tennessee, 22 December 1863, a part of the orders reads as follows, "Maj. Gen. James S. Negley, U.S. Volunteers, is hereby directed to proceed to Cincinnati, or to any point outside this military division, and report by letter to the Adjutant-General of the Army for orders."[86] Against these orders, as casting reflections upon him, General Negley made strong complaint to General George H. Thomas, in a letter of 11 January 1864.[87]

In the Court of Inquiry before which General Negley was tried, late in January 1864, his actions at Chickamauga were fully explained and he was completely exonerated of all charges, while one of his accusing critics, Brigadier General Thomas J. Wood, was sharply censured for his own shortcomings on the battlefield of Chickamauga.[88]

Exoneration was not followed by restoration to command in the field. In vain, General Negley held himself in readiness. From Louisville, Kentucky, on 30 March 1864, he wrote General Sherman as follows:

General: Encouraged by your former kindness to me, and the fact that you are familiar with my services and efficiency as a commander, I am induced to solicit a command in your department. I am confident that if you make the request it will be granted. You are doubtless aware of the injustice I have suffered and that I fully vindicated my reputation before the court of inquiry. Your friendly consideration of this request will place me under personal obligations.[89]

Since there is no record of a reply to this letter and General Negley was never restored to command, it is apparent that the injustice done him was never remedied.[90]

It is possible and even probable that General Negley's treatment was a result of that well-known rivalry of West Pointers and civilian commanders which has characterized all the warfare of the United States since the establishment of that famous academy.[91] For example, General Sheridan, a West Pointer, suffered no such treatment as General Negley although his behavior at Chickamauga was somewhat identical.[92] Certainly in later life, General Negley was bitter against West Point influence in the army and on politics.[93]

On his retirement to Pittsburgh and private life, General Negley resided for a year in Collins Township.[94] In 1865, his residence was on Center Avenue, near Shadyside, East Liberty. He continued to reside in Shadyside during the remainder of his residence in Pittsburgh.[95] From 1869 to 1886, he appears to have resided on Ellsworth Avenue, but in the latter year he changed his residence to Fifth Avenue, near Highland Avenue.[96]

General Negley's untoward fate in the army does not appear to have injured his standing with his fellow citizens in Western Pennsylvania. In 1868 he was nominated and elected to Congress on the Republican ticket. On taking his seat in the Forty-first Congress, he was, in its first session, placed on the Committee on Enrolled Bills.[97] Very early in the session he introduced a bill to reduce the number of officers in the army of the United States,[98] a matter which indicates both his attitude toward the army and his support of efficiency and economy. In such a matter he was carrying over into his legislative career the influence of his experience in military life.

In politics, Congressman Negley was a stout upholder of the policies of the post-bellum Republican Party and an earnest advocate of the interests of his constituency. In the second session of the Forty-first Congress, he presented a large number of petitions from his constituents.[99] The most significant of these were those in favor of the maintenance of a protective tariff on iron products and those against imported cigars. The suspicion is inescapable that not all such petitions were wholly voluntary, that some of them were instigated. Negley's own support of the protective tariff policy is demonstrated by a long speech in its defense, 17 March 1870,[100] and by a shorter speech of the same type about one month later.[101] But in this same session he manifested an interest in commerce and transportation,[102] subjects in which he was to retain interest during the remainder of his life. He also worked for a soldier's monument in Allegheny Park,[103] and, as occasion offered, was active in the interests of disabled soldiers.[104]

In the first session of the Forty-second Congress, the main activity of Congressman Negley was the presentation of a bill to make Pittsburgh a federal port of entry. Passage of the bill was refused and the bill was referred to the Committee on Commerce.[105] Congressman Samuel J. Randall, the famous Pennsylvania Democrat, was largely responsible for this setback,[106] but the bill was the forerunner of important activities along this line by Congressman Negley in later sessions.

A total of 32 bills were introduced by Negley in the second session of this Congress.[107] On one day, 15 January 1872, among other bills, he submitted a bill for the purchase of a suitable site and the erection of a satisfactory federal building in Pittsburgh; a bill for the establishment in Pittsburgh of an adequate marine hospital; a bill for the improvement of the Ohio River; and a bill for the improvement of the Monongahela River.[108] In this session, he also presented numerous petitions from members of his constituency, of which petitions 18 or more were in support of the protective tariff, several in favor of relief from restrictions on steam pressure in the boilers of towboats, and two or more in behalf of bounty legislation for federal soldiers.[109]

On 29 February 1872, he made a short but strong speech defending Colonel T.A. Scott, president of the Pennsylvania Railroad (and the friend of Andrew Carnegie) against criticism made upon him by a congressional speaker.[110] At this time, Negley was seemingly on the Committee on Commerce. Early in March he reported from this committee a bill moderating restrictions on steam pressure in the boilers of tow boats not carrying passengers.[111] With much difficulty he succeeded in having the bill called up for consideration on 25 March 1872,[112] and after serious debate and many amendments, kept on the schedule.[113] A week later he secured the passage by the House of Representatives of a bill, reported from the Committee on Commerce, providing for improvements in the Ohio River in aid of navigation.[114] In the midst of this activity in regard to transportation he found opportunity to make a brief protective tariff speech on 16 May 1872.[115] While, in this session, he failed to secure the passage of the tow boat steam-pressure bill, he did secure the passage of a bill appropriating $300,000 for the purchase of a site for a new federal building at Pittsburgh.[116]

In the third session of the Forty-second Congress, Negley introduced seven bills, among them illustrating his interest in transportation. These included a bill, on 9 December 1872, to complete a waterway from tidewater on the James River to the Ohio River at the mouth of the Kanawha, and, on 16 December 1872, a railroad bill. On the latter date he also presented a memorial on the improvement of the Ohio River.[117] In addition he secured consent to print a long speech on internal navigation in which he set forth vigorously the advantages of water way competition with railroads.[118]

In the Forty-third Congress, Negley was again put on the Committee on Commerce and also placed upon the Committee on Mines and Mining.[119] In the first session he introduced 31 bills, among them a bill for a marine hospital at Pittsburgh, a bill for improving the Monongahela River, and a bill for improving the Ohio River.[120] Among the 21 petitions from his constituents presented by him, were a petition from druggists in favor of the repeal of stamp taxes on medicines,[121] a petition of 900 church members for an investigation of the liquor trade,[122] and six protective tariff petitions.[123] Negley in this session of Congress,[124] was one of those who upheld the act of the previous session which increased the pay of members of Congress, an act commonly known as the "salary grab." A matter of bitter recrimination in Congress and in the newspapers of the time, this act has usually, though not always, been condemned by historians.

However, apart from some attention to land grants and mining rights in the West, resulting from one of his committee appointments,[125] Congressman Negley's main interest remained in commerce and transportation. On 8 December 1873, he secured the passage of a bill permitting 150 pounds instead of a maximum of 110 pounds steam-pressure on tow boats.[126] On 30 March 1874, he made a short speech in behalf of a canal on the Ohio River at the falls near Louisville, Kentucky.[127] In May, 1874, he made a long speech in relation to security of life on steam vessels in which he displayed not only great knowledge of the problems of shipping on inland rivers, but considerable familiarity with legal precedents bearing on the matter.[128] A bill dealing with such shipping was finally carried through the House of Representatives, on 13 May 1874.[129] Negley was also instrumental in this session in securing the passage of a bill giving the Allegheny Valley Railroad right of way through the grounds of the United States Arsenal at Pittsburgh.[130]

In the second session of the Forty-third Congress, Negley introduced 11 bills, among them three for improvements of the Allegheny, Monongahela, and Ohio Rivers;[131] two in regard to a railroad in Utah;[132] one for the construction of a bridge at St. Louis, Missouri;[133] and another for the construction of a bridge at Monroe, Louisiana.[134] Among other petitions he presented two from Pittsburgh in regard to improvements on the rivers,[135] and one for the repeal of the 10 percent reduction in tariff duties, which had been made in 1872.[136] Against his protests the bill for a bridge at St. Louis was severely amended,[137] and nothing came of his work for his other bills. In keeping with his strong Republican Party principles, when the famous Force Bill in regard to federal supervision of elections came up at this session, Negley spoke in its advocacy.[138] But for a decade he was to be absent from the halls of Congress, and his first period of Congressional service came to an end with the expiration of the session in March 1875.

The retired general and ex-Congressman was for the next 10 years a prominent citizen of Pittsburgh, mainly engaged in business but not without interest in other local matters. It was during this period that, in 1877, he served in command of local armed forces organized in Pittsburgh for the control of the mobs in the famous railroad riots.[139] According to one of the many accessible biographical sketches[140] of General Negley, "In the early seventies, General Negley turned his attention to business affairs. He conceived and planned the Pittsburgh and Western railroad, was interested in the construction of the Nickel Plate Railroad and a smaller railroad in Ohio. Negley, Ohio, through which one of his railroads runs, was named after him."[141] In 1878, General Negley is listed in the Pittsburgh Directory as "vice pres't.

Pitts. New Castle & Lake Erie R.R., Seventh Av. and Smithfield."[142] In 1882, he is listed as "Pres't. N.Y.P. & C. Ry. Co., Seventh Av. and Smithfield."[143] In addition, during the period from 1878 until 1885, Negley held the position of gas inspector in Pittsburgh.[144] Assisting him in his railway enterprises during these years was his son, James S. Negley, Jr., who served as secretary for one of the railroads in which his father was interested.[145]

In 1884, General Negley was again elected to Congress. Almost his first activity in the first session of the Forty-ninth Congress was the introduction of bills for the improvement of the Allegheny, Ohio and Monongahela Rivers.[146] In April, he made a stout effort to secure by amendment an increase from $40,000 to $140,000 in the appropriation for improvement of the Allegheny River, but without success.[147] In this Congress, in keeping with his military record, Congressman Negley was put on the Committee on Military Affairs.[148] As in former sessions of Congress, Negley stands forth from the records, a champion of stalwart Republicanism and of the interests of his constituency. He presented a petition against the passage of the Morrison Tariff bill[149] and no less than nine petitions of window glass workers against the revision of the existing tariff.[150] His vote was regularly cast against any motion intended to facilitate revision of the existing tariff.[151] In keeping with the Republican principle of the sacredness of private property, General Negley made a vigorous but vain effort to secure federal compensation to James Mellinger of Pittsburgh for property which was destroyed in Nashville, Tennessee, during the Civil War.[152] He also vigorously opposed a bill which would have taken over the works of the Monongahela Navigation Company at $20,000 or less,[153] and voted against a bill to forfeit land grants to the Northern Pacific Railroad.[154] For some reason which is not clear, General Negley made a long speech[155] against the Congressional bill for the relief of General Fitz John Porter from the charges made against him in 1862, and voted with the minority against the bill at the time of its passage.[156]

But the two most notable aspects of the activity of Congressman Negley in this session are the accentuation of his interest in old soldiers and an interest in progressive social legislation. He introduced a bill to compensate the National Home for Disabled Volunteer Soldiers at Phoebus, Virginia, for losses due to a bank failure in Norfolk, Virginia,[157] and finally secured the passage of the bill by the House of Representatives.[158] And he introduced a bill constituting 10 hours a day's work for all conductors and drivers employed on the street railways in the District of Columbia.[159]

In the second session, Congressman Negley presented at least four petitions asking for the reduction or repeal of internal taxes.[160] He voted against measures bearing on tariff reduction.[161] His old interests are seen in his bill permitting the construction of the Hotel Chamberlain at Fortress Monroe, Virginia,[162] and his bill granting a right of way and other privileges to the Hampton and Old Point Railroad Company.[163] His interest in old soldiers was maintained.[164] But in line with his interest in reform, he presented a petition "for national aid to common schools, from citizens of Pittsburgh, Pa."[165] and voted in favor of the bill for the establishment of a Department of Agriculture in the federal government.[166]

But General Negley's days in Congress were already numbered and coming to an end. In the nomination convention of 1886 he had been defeated by John Dalzell,[167] who was elected from the Twenty-second District in November[168] and continuously re-elected for the next quarter of a century.[169]

On his retirement from Congress, General Negley appears to have quickly given up residence in Pittsburgh.[170] In connection with his railroad interests, he seems to have organized the Railroad Supply Company and moved his headquarters to New York City.[171] His home was made in Plainfield, New Jersey, from which he went daily to his offices in Liberty Street, New York.[172] And in Plainfield, New Jersey, he died on 7 August 1901.[173] The date is important, for on his splendid tombstone in the Allegheny Cemetery, it is erroneously inscribed that he "Died 12 August 1901."

His body was brought back to Pittsburgh. The funeral services were conducted by Dr. William J. Holland, formerly the pastor of the Bellefield Presbyterian Church,[174] and burial took place in the Negley family burial plot in the Allegheny Cemetery.

One obituary stated that "General Negley was a man of large physique, being six feet high and well built."[175] It is also said that "He was an indefatigable worker and carried to success everything he undertook."[176] It is the testimony of those who knew him well,[177] that General Negley was urbane, polite and gentlemanly, but affable and friendly; moderately well-to-do, but not rich; independent in spirit but loyal to his friends and constituents; and withal a striking man in personal appearance. As an indication of his esteem among his contemporaries, it may be noted that "For fifteen years he was one of the managers of the National Home for Volunteers, was president of the National Union League of America, and was active in the Grand Army of the Republic and other military organizations."[178]

General Negley was twice married. In 1848, he married Kate Losey by whom he had three sons, Clifford, James S., and George. If the date on the tombstone is accurate, his first wife died 30 November 1867. None of his three sons by his first wife survived General Negley.[179] In middle life he married Grace Ashton,[180] who was 23 years his junior, by whom he had three daughters, Grace, Edith, and Mabel. Of these daughters, Grace married Enoch S. Farson and had two sons, James

Negley Farson and Enoch S. Farson. According to the inscription on the tombstone, his second wife survived him by a quarter of a century, dying 1 July 1927.

His descendants still living no longer reside in Pittsburgh. But many collateral relatives continue to live in the old family neighborhood, some of whom yet remember one of their most distinguished members. And wherever his relatives may be, they have in General Negley's record little for which to apologize, nothing which is inexplicable, and much of which to be proud. ★

CHAPTER 5

A BUCKTAIL VOICE: CIVIL WAR CORRESPONDENCE OF PRIVATE CORDELLO COLLINS

EDITED BY MARK REINSBERG

Biographies of prominent officers tend to neglect another important element of Western Pennsylvania's role in the Civil War — the lives of the everyday soldiers who fought, and died, in the service of the commonwealth. In his contribution to this volume, Mark Reinsberg uses a collection of letters written by a young enlistee from Warren County to his relatives on the home front to provide a compelling portrait of the day-to-day experiences of a typical Western Pennsylvania soldier. (Soldiers in his regiment, the 42nd Pennsylvania, attached bucktails to their hats as a sign of marksmanship.) The letters, though literarily unrefined, are invaluable historical documents as they reveal, first-hand, the tedium of camp life, the relationships that existed between soldiers and their officers, the trials and tribulations of infantry duties, and — perhaps most importantly — the many horrors of Civil War combat. This essay was first published in the July 1965 issue of *Western Pennsylvania Historical Magazine.*

Left: An unidentified member of the Bucktail regiment. From the collection of the McKean County Historical Society, reproduced in *Bucktailed Wildcats* by Edwin A. Glover (1960). — HSWP Library & Archives, Library collection

T HESE ARE THE LETTERS OF A YOUNG SOLDIER FROM WARREN COUNTY, Pennsylvania, who served as a rifleman in the original Bucktail Regiment[1] from the outbreak of the Rebellion until wounded and left behind in a Gettysburg hospital. The letters were written to his parents and younger brothers and sisters, and there was a note also to the daughter of a neighbor. Unpublished except for one piece that appeared in the *Warren Mail* in 1862, this correspondence was preserved in the soldier's pension file in the National Archives, Washington, D.C.

Cordello Collins was 21 years old and unmarried at the time of his enlistment in the elite company recruited by Captain (eventually Brigadier General) Roy Stone known as the "Raftsmen's Guard."[2] The marksmanship of a hunter and the hardiness of a lumberman were the standards for enrollment in this Warren County group, and Collins easily qualified. He was an excellent shot, having, like most of the Raftsmen, handled a gun in the backwoods since childhood. He was a sturdy, blue-eyed youth of five-foot-eight, toughened in limb by his apprenticeship as a blacksmith, and several winters of lumbering.

The Collinses were insolvent. Cordello's dollar-a-day earnings in the lumber woods had gone to the support of his parents, as did a substantial portion of his army pay. The latter circumstance, as we shall see, preserved the correspondence.

The Collins family had migrated to Pennsylvania from New York in the early 1840s. They lived in the village of Kinzua, on the Allegheny River, where John Collins, Cordello's father, had set up as a blacksmith. For a time, Mr. Collins could afford to keep two assistants in his shop. Ultimately, Kinzua was an unlucky choice of location. The area had been celebrated for its pine forest, but by the Civil War period lumbering in Kinzua had declined. The number of households engaged in farming had also declined.[3] Moreover, there were three other blacksmiths competing for business in the village, and hardly 400 souls in the entire township.

The family possessed a few acres of cleared land and two cows. John Collins, approaching 60, was heavily in debt. His health began to fail during the war years, until he lay bedridden. His wife Dolly, a Vermont woman with eight children to provide for besides her invalid husband, would be reduced to taking in washing[4] while her eldest son defended the Union.

In editing Private Collins' letters I have intruded only so far as to supply initial capitals and periods, and a few paragraph indentations. I have made a point of retaining the misspellings, not to exhibit the soldier's limitations, but because of the clues they occasionally have to the pronunciations of the Pennsylvania Wildcat region in the mid-19th century. [The term "Wildcat" was commonly used to describe Pennsylvania's lumbering region. Lumbermen were nicknamed "Wildcats" for their rough hewn, frontier ways].

Admittedly, the letters of Cordello Collins have no literary merit whatsoever. Their formal historical value may also be slight. And yet, they are affecting to read. And they give us social insight that is beyond the reach of commentary.

"I Want You to Send Me a Bucktail"
November th 1 1861
Camp Pierpoint
Fairfax Co. Va.

Dear Perrants

I received your letter day before yesterday. It was dated the 23 of Oct. I was glad to hear from you and that you was so well there. You wrote to me that you herd that the Pa. solgers was all killed in that hard fite[5] but noe of the Pa. Solgers was there. That paper will tell you all I know about it. I have sent 3 news papers there. I wrote one letter the 11 or 12 of Oct. I don't know whitch. I have received 5 letters from you. I don't know how meny letters I have wrote to you but now I am goin to put down every one I write and the day of the month.

We have had 4 or 5 hard frosts heare. Last night was very cold heare but was cloudy. Last Monday and teusday we had a genral in spection. The bucktails had the prais of bein the best drilled regment out of the Pa. reserve V.C. Yesterday our regiment had a genral muster.

We expect 2 month pay now. I have sined my name to the Capt roal to have $6.00 dollars per month sent to you. I direcked it to mother. For I did not know but if I sent it to you father that some one you oad would try to get it. This money will be sent to judge R. Brown[6] at Warren. You myst go there to get it. Or send a order for it. There will be 12 dollars now sent. And maby it will be 2 month be fore it will come again but look out for it. It will be 12 dollars every 2 monnth. Save every cent of this mony to pay for a home for you and nothing elce. For my sake. When you pay this moy out be shure it wont be lost. Pay it out in mothers or my name. So you can keep it. I have 7 dollars left to me heare per month. That is a nuf for me to use a month.

While I am heare we have had one Skirmish heare. The 20 of Oct. some of this rement had fire one shot a piece at them and killed 4 or 5 of the Secess hourse men about 3/4 of a mile. This is all I can think of now at presant. Only we have got a new suit of close. There are a first rate suit. They are a dark blue collar. The coat is a frock coat worth a bout 8 dollars.

This song, let one of the boys lern it and speak it to school.[7] We will have songs better than this after a while but this is the truth. When you write let me know if you got them papers, 3 of them. And I sent Amy a song. Tell me if she got that. It Cost me 15 cents for 5 and they ask 5 cents for 1 and this Song costs 3 cents.

I want you to send me a bucktail.[8] Put a paper a round it and sent it by mail. Or if you can find Juit[9] at Warren you can send it by him if he comes back again. I would like to have one from home for the naim of it.

Write how much snow there has binn there and if you has killed eny dear since I came from home. The 19th, the Pa. solgers marched about 18 miles out in to wards manasas gap. Then we laid down for to stay over night but about 9 oclock we was ordered back 2 miles to the Cross roads to where the most of the regements was. Then stade there over night and Sonday till Monday. Then marched back to our camps Monday. We have had a peaceiful time since then heare but we expect to move from heare soon.

We have a nuf to eat heare sutch as it is. But I have to buy some sweet potatoes and py and sweet cakes, butter Chease and apples to suit my taste. Butter is from 25 to 30 Cents a pount. Chease from 15 to 20 Cents per pound. Sweet potatoes 5 Cents per pound. Are [following line crossed out: Juit is come I spoke of at Warren.] I am well at present and harty. I can lay the sweet potatoes and butter down to a pritty good advantage. But Flectcher Hamlin[10] can beat me eating. But we have plenty now. Apples at the sise of them sweet ones would sell heare too for 5 cents. I give yesterday 5 cents for one apple about the sise of a cup or your best.

Write to me soon as you can. I reming your affectionare Friend.

Cordello Collins

Write as before

John Collins
Dolly Collins

"If I Git Cortmarchal for It"

Jan. the 26 1862

[Camp Pierpont]

Dear Perrants

I now take my pen in hand to inform that I am a live and midlin well. I have got a small cold and my head akes a little but I dont think it will last long.

I just sent 20 dollars by express to Mrs Dolly Collins at Kinzua. It will be left at Warren with Judge R. Brown. That will be besides the 12 that the govament send. 12 dollars more is to be sent there now. Look out for it all. 12 that was there, 12 that goes there this time and 20 I sent you by express. Look out for that mony. I think that is a nuf to pay for loozin a day for.

> 12
> 12
> 20
> ―――
> $44 Dollars

I expect mother you will have to give pap an order to git it for I sent it in your name so no one would take it for debt. Git it soon as you can for you dont know how I feel about it. Because you hant got that 12 dollars that has been there so long and I want you to try to git that mony rite off. And let me know if you can git it or not, for if you cant I want to know it so I can try and stop it. But I dont expect I can. But if you cant git it I shall try to stop it if I git cortmarchal for it. Write soon and let me know all a bout it for I feel uneazy a bout it.

We expect to move from heare soon and I dont know where we will go but I expect it will be to South Carolina. It is re ported that we shall march from hear with in 10 days but I dont know how true it is. Sylvester he is at Baltimore in the Genral hospitle.[11] Fletcher is in the Hospitle at Gorgetown. I got a letter from Sylvester night be fore last. He says he is no better than he was when he left Camp. No more.

Truly yours

Cordello

John Collins
Dolly Collins
Dolly
Dolly

Cordello Collins
Union forever[12]

"We Slaughtered Them Big"

[Reprinted from the *Warren Mail*, 23 August 1862, this letter was obviously edited for publication.]

Camp of the Bucktails. 1st Rifles,
Harrison's Landing [Va.]
July 19, '62

Dear Parents: — I received a letter from you yesterday, dated July the 8th. It gave me the greatest of pleasure to hear that you were all well. My health is as good as usual and my shoulder almost well.

We are camped on land that formerly belonged to President Harrison, on James River. I suppose that you have heard in Kenzua that the rebels were mowing us down right and left, but we gave them as good as they gave us, you had better believe. We killed three or four of them to where they killed one of us, although they outnumbered us three to one – they were so drunk they shot over us. But let me tell you it was a hot place; I don't fancy the place at all; it seemed impossible for anybody to live a minute, but thank the Lord we were able to pay them in their own coin. Our Regiment fought four days in the seven days fight.

On Thursday, when the fighting commenced,[13] our company had the first shot at the enemy made by our infantry. We were in the edge of the woods behind a fence — the rebels out in the field about ten or fifteen rods off in four ranks marching broadside. We took a rest from the fence and trees and fired. Oh! You ought to have seen them jump up and fall; they did not see us at all, altho' they were on three sides of us. We had now to fall back to our rifle pits and then there was war in the camp in earnest; the fight had actually begun. I laid in our rifle pits right under the mount of one of our own cannons.[14] Sometimes I thought I should go entirely deaf. Four shells came into our pits where our company was; three of them we flung out before they bursted; the other went into the bank behind us and exploded, though fortunately nobody was injured.

The enemy charged bayonets on us three times, but we cut them down with such a galling fire that they ran back much faster than they came. I fired until my gun got so hot that I could hardly hold it in my hands, and I had to stop to let it cool. On the first day one of our companies, Co. K, was surrounded and taken prisoners before they could get to their rifle pits. The night of the first day we slept in our pits. The next morning the battle was renewed and old Stonewall Jackson was flanking us, and we had to leave the pits and fall back and take a new position. When this order was given, Company E, and the greater part of our company [D] did not hear the order and were left and the rebels got them. That afternoon they came on us again.[15] We laid in the open fields and the rebels mostly in the woods; this was a hard fight; we slaughtered them big, and they killed a great many of us; the ground was spotted with dead rebels. Here I was wounded with a piece of shell, and it seems like a miracle that I got out alive. It was just a buzz, whizz, and all kinds of noise from grape and canister balls and slam bang of bursting shells all around and over our heads, killing me on all sides. Saturday and Monday [remainder of this line of type illegible in microfilm print] Monday was equal to Friday, but I was not engaged for I could not use my left arm.

Thursday night after the firing had ceased, we could hear the wounded rebels cry for help and asking for some one to bring them a drink of water and calling on the Maker to help them. It seemed the most pityful of anything I ever heard or seen to hear the different sounds and moans over the ground. — Some seemed to be in awful agony; but they had to lay there without any one to give them water or help in the least.

I will now close by observing that it was through the help of the Lord that I escaped so well, and I devoutly thank him for it. Please write soon.[16]

From your affectionate son,
Cordello Collins

"We Have Had Hard Times"
Camp Bucktails[17]
Sept 4 /62

Dear Mother
I received a letter from you last night. I was glad to hear from you and to hear your health was so good. My health is midling good.

We have had hard times lately. For about 2 weeks we have had to march every day hard and had 3 fights. Fought three battles in the time. Last thirsday friday and Saturday all day hard.[18]

We had 1 days ration of food to last the 3 days. I was the nearist dun out then that I ever was.[19] I could hardly stand a lone but I had to keep a going. I hant got over it yet. You can see that by my writing. I hant but a time to write now. I will write soon and let you know all the perticlers. I came through the fights safe and sound.

We have got new guns, the Sharps rifles, the best guns out. Lods in the brich and caps its self. I can load in 5 seconds and keep it up.[20]

Tell me if you have got the $12 dollars from Warren lately since you got the 57 dollars. Now I will close.

Your dear sun

Cordello

PS tell Phebe I greately thank her for the Warren Mail.

"McDowel[21] Let Them Flank Us"

[This letter is undated but accompanied letter of Sept. 4, 1862]

Dear Friend Susan

I received the letter you wrote to me with the greatest of plesure. I was very glad to hear from home and from my nabors.

We are now on Arlington hights near Washington. It is very likely we will stay here and recrute up again.

We have had some very hard fighting on the same old battle ground at Bulls run. The rebels flanked us and we had to fall back but we whiped them in frunt and was driving them when the order came to fall back.

I was in 3 different battles there. We drove them every time tho there. But Mcdowel let them flank us so we had to fall back to the rear.

It is very hard work for me to write now for I am tired and nervis and have to write on my knees and set on the ground. So I will clos. Write soon.

From your Friend

Cordello Collins

To Susen English[22]
With my pen I write the same
Cordello Collins in my name
The pen is blind and couldent see
So blaime the pen and don't blame me.

"Alass and We Lost Our Col."

Camp Bucktails[23]

Sept 22 1862

Dear pearants

I now take my pen in hand to inform you that I am yet a live and well. We have seen 3 days more of hard fighting. 4 killed out of our Co. D. Sargent Trask private Cob and Henry Glasier from Corydon is dead and Stewart. And 7 wounded, Nelt Gear in the Right brest mortely.[24]

The 14 day we comence fighting on South hill [Turner's Gap on South Mountain, near the battlefield at Antietem]. The rebel ocupide the side of the behind rocks and Stone walls while we took the flat. But we chaised them over the mounting and slauted [slaughtered] them big. There 1 was killed 3 wounded of our Co. D.

The 15th we laid over. The 16 fought again: 3 killed and 4 wounded of our Co. The 17 none hurt of our Co.

William Kibby was killed from Kinzua.[25] Steven Harris is wounded in the hand. He is in the 10 Regment. Our Regt lost more men in this battle than we ever did at once before.

Alass and we lost out Col. McNeil. The 16 he was shot through the hart.[26] We hant got but 2 captins in our regt. One of them act as Col.[27]

Oh Dear parents we day before yesterday we came a cross a part of the battle field where the dead laid so thick a man could step from one to a nother without eny trouble at all. Some places they laid a cross each other and they was swelled so they looked more like some kind of wild brutes than men and black as nigars. Oh how horable it did look. Some shot in the head in the boddy. Some both lages of lost up and some mangel in the most harabel maner that can be thought. They was mostly secesh.

But we want in that fight there. Our Regt has the best guns in the U.S. Brich loders and self capers.

All the kinds of fish we could catch this summer was catfish and bass sunfish eels herrins and perch.

Tell me where Leeorren Labree is and how to write to him.[28]

Tell me if you got the last $12 I sent to you.

I will not close by abserving that it is through the help of the Lord that I yet live. Write soon.

Your sun
Cordello Collins
Cordello Collins
Cordello

Hear is 25 cents

"We Whiped Our Selfs"

Camp Near Bells plains [Va.]
January the 28 63

Dear Mother

My letter hant gone yet that I wrote yesterday and we have got order that we are goin to Washington to do pervose duty. So you see that is the reason that I did scratch out the direckions. Direct the Box as I said first, Cordello Collins Co. D first Rifles Bucktails Regt. P.R.V.C. Care of Lieut. Hall Washington D.C.

We have after so long a time we have got 4 munths pay. 24 Dollars of it goes home as usual by the U.S. express. Please go rite down and see about getting it and go to Oris Hall and get my revolver.

If Robert Campbell[29] can wait till a nother payment is made to me please keep that monny to pay for things that I want acasionaly in the time of nead and to by stamps for me and uther things as I send for them. And I want some to use when I get my discharge. Use of the monney all you want to use to make out the express box or to by stamps to send your letters.

The snow is the deepest now that I have seen it since I left Penna. It is 8 or 10 inches deep. The sun is shining now very bright.

Mr. Oris Hall[30] did not go home the other day so he is goin to day I believe.

We have pretty happy little meetings here in my tent. I am pointed a clase leader of our little meeting. We call it the name of Christon Soldier. There is 5 in the Class of us:" Gorge W. Chase, Gorge W. Gates, Fletcher Hamlin, Frederick Knup [Knopf]. Thoses is the name of the ones that belong to the class and myself. The too first ones is the ones that tents with me. That is all of this.

Well now a little more of Burnsides movement. If it had not been for the rain perhaps we would whiped the secesh very bad but through the luck we whiped our selfs.[31] No more of this. Write soon.

From your affectionate Sun

Cordello Collins

To Mr. John Collins

And to Mrs Dolly Collins   Dolly Collins

Cordello Collins

"The Best Shot Gets a Preamem"

Camp 1st Rifles[32]

Apr 29 [1863]

Dearest Pearants

I received a letter from you and Amy to day. It gave me the greatest of pleasure. I was very glad to hear from you but I was sorrow to hear that you pap was so aling in your lungs.

I am well and harty. I belive I could eat ten or twelve morinoess taters if I could get them. I way one hundred and seventy five pounds. 175 lbs and on picket every 2nd or 3rd day and night rain or shine. That is what makes us grow so.

I got 4 munths pay to day. You can see by Johns and Nancys letters.

The camp guard fires off ther guns every morning at a mark and the one that makes the best shot gets a preamem of 50 cents. I have been on guard twice since that has been the order and I got the half dollar both times. We shot 250 yards then but we shoot 300 yeards now. Both of my shots would hit a deers head. I shot one day once at a mark on a tree 200 steps or yards and hit over the senter about a half of an inch. I belive I can hit a deers head 200 yards every time if I could guess the rite distent. Well I will close this. Rite soon.

Your affectionate sun
Cordello Collins

To John and Dolly Collins

Send me some Stamps

"I May Come Home This Somer"

Camp 1st Rifles

April 29/63

Dear Johny and Nancy

I now take the present opportunity to answer your kind letters. I got a letter to day from pap and Amy. Pap said you both was very anctious to get a letter from me in reply to yourn. I thought that I had answerd your letter before but if I hant you must excuse me this time. I hant mutch news to tell you this time. Only that the trees is in flow[er] here. The grass is growing fast. It is raining here now.

I got 4 mounths pay to day. 24 dollars goes home as usual by the U.S.

John I expect your steers is old whoppers. Oh I wish I was there now but I ant so there is no use of wishing. But I hope it will be so that I may come home this somer eather for good or on a visett.

Nancy you can write pretty well. You can all most beat Amy a writing. Johny you hant lernt so fast lately as you did. Can Ebby write eny yet?

I sent the roll of our Company as it is now home. The names that has the star to is the ones that has been wounded & C. Write soon.

Your affectionate Brother

Cordello Collins

There were, obviously, other letters in this correspondence which were not preserved.

About a year-and-a-half after this letter, Cordello's father, John Collins, died in Kinzua of tuberculosis. His wife Dolly was left in impoverished circumstances, with four or five children still to raise.

Some time after the Civil War, Mrs. Collins made application to the U.S. Commissioner of Pensions. As proof that her deceased son Cordello had contributed substantially to the family support while in the army, she submitted these letters which discussed money matters. And as a consequence this part of the wartime correspondence was preserved in the soldier's pension file.

Cordello Collins had been desperately wounded at Gettysburg on 3 July 1863. The Bucktails had fought in the Wheatfield and opposite Devil's Den on 2 July 1863, and through the next day they helped to hold Little Round Top, counterattacking after the defeat of Pickett's Charge.

For the next month, Collins made a stubborn fight for his life in Two Taverns Hospital, dying at last of his wounds on 8 August 1863.

Careless record-keeping and high cumulative casualties in the Bucktail Regiment deprived Collins of his modest share of posthumous glory. When the unit was mustered out of the service in June 1864, there was apparently no one left who remembered Cordello or, in any case, no one who reminded the regimental clerk of his fate. In the official records he was listed as "Not on muster-out roll." ★

SOME ASPECTS OF PITTSBURGH'S INDUSTRIAL CONTRIBUTIONS TO THE CIVIL WAR

BY LOUIS VAIRA

Western Pennsylvania's contribution to the American Civil War constituted much more than supplying the soldiers who filled the ranks of its cavalry, infantry, and artillery regiments. The region, particularly the city of Pittsburgh, also made a profound industrial impact on the Union war effort. In fact, the city was so important as a commercial and industrial center that fear of its capture led to a coordinated effort to fortify the city from possible Confederate raids of military stockpiles. In this essay, Louis Vaira examines Pittsburgh's overall industrial contribution to the Civil War, including its production of iron plating for the Union Navy's fledgling ironclad fleet and the fabrication of some of the largest cannons then known. This paper was originally read before the Historical Society of Western Pennsylvania on 31 May 1922 and was published in the January 1923 issue of *Western Pennsylvania Historical Magazine*.

Left: One of the giant 15-inch Rodman Columbiad cannons (popularly known as the "Lincoln Gun"), produced at Pittsburgh's Fort Pitt Foundry, watches over Fort Monroe, Hampton Roads, Virginia. — Library of Congress

P ITTSBURGH AS AN INDUSTRIAL AND COMMERCIAL CENTER IS TODAY universally known. Its position among the cities of the United States is unique. As a manufacturing center it is more noted since the products particularly of the steel mills are shipped to all parts of the world. Such epithets as "Smoky City," "Steel City" and the "Birmingham of America" bear witness to the fact.

The above could not be said of Pittsburgh prior to the Civil War. At that time it was known as the "Key to the West," being the appropriate name given by those hardy, restless pioneers, who were tired of eastern aristocracy and desired a better home in the democratic west. Still, the position of Pittsburgh as the "Key to the West" remains, but far different is her present position as such. It is no longer a pathway whereby settlers can enter the virgin forest and field of the west, but on the other hand is a point where many other cities buy their supplies.

At the time when the Southern States were seriously contemplating secession, Pittsburgh would seem, to the average person today, to be in a precarious position. It had been accustomed to shipping coal, iron, agricultural implements, and other products to the South. It would have been, therefore, not unnatural for its inhabitants and businessmen to at least sympathize with the seceding states. Nothing, however, could be farther from the truth.

Immediately after the election of President Abraham Lincoln, the Southern States started on a period of gigantic seizure of government property. This began with the seizure of forts and arsenals, which were located within the boundaries of the dissatisfied states. Then, with many Southern supporters of states rights in the cabinet of President James Buchanan, much ordnance and other munitions of war were shipped south. This was particularly true of the Secretary of War, John B. Floyd. Mainly through his efforts several northern arsenals were relieved of much of their supplies, which were ordered south.

Among the victims of such an order was the Allegheny Arsenal, located in the Lawrenceville section of Pittsburgh. An order was received by Major John Symington, officer in charge of the arsenal, to ship 100, 20-pound guns to New Orleans, destined for Texas. The order was received on 23 December 1860.[1] The moment this order became known to the people much excitement resulted. A petition, signed by a number of influential citizens was sent to the mayor requesting him to call for a public meeting for the purpose of preventing the removal of the guns.

The commander of the arsenal failed to give a satisfactory answer as to the destination of the guns. As a result, a meeting was called for 27 December; where a committee composed of Messrs. Wilkins, Shaler, Robinson, and Williams read an order addressed to President Buchanan.[2] Excitement ran high. After passing a few resolutions expressing indignation and injustice at the removal of guns, the meeting adjourned.

Excitement went a pitch higher when James K. Moorhead received an answer to his telegram sent to Edwin M. Stanton, Chairman of the Committee of Military Affairs, to the effect that the shipment of the guns was to be prevented.[3] A contract had been made with the *Silver Wave* to carry the guns to New Orleans,[4] and the guns were being hauled to the wharf, when the above answer was received. Plans were prepared for the forceful prevention of the removal of the guns, when the Floyd order was countermanded, 3 January,[5] and further trouble was avoided. These happenings clearly show that Pittsburgh was anything but in favor of secession.

As has been stated before, Pittsburgh was considered the "Key to the West." It would, therefore, be of great value to ascertain Pittsburgh's efforts in helping to withstand the Confederate attack in the west and its contributions to this end.

In this respect the spotlight is turned on Colonel Charles Ellet's Ram Fleet, which was a part of the Mississippi Flotilla. It was the object of the flotilla to cooperate with the land forces under Ulysses S. Grant. It was Ellet's purpose to repulse the rebel ironclads around Memphis, Island No. 10, and other southern strongholds.[6]

With this end in view, Ellet purchased five of the nine boats, which were to constitute his fleet, at Pittsburgh. These were the *Lioness, Sampson* and *Mingo*, "three powerful Ohio river stern-wheel tow-boats," and the *Fulton* and *Homer*, "two small stern-wheel tow-boats, as tender and dispatch boat for the fleet."[7] In addition to these, one battery barge was also purchased here. Ellet, in making his report to Commodore Andrew Foote, refers to the Pittsburgh tugs as "three of the strongest and swiftest stern-wheel coal tow-boats."[8]

These were obtained as a result of instructions from Edwin Stanton, by then Lincoln's Secretary of War, issued on 27 March 1862, which ordered Ellet to proceed immediately to Pittsburgh, Cincinnati, and New Albany and take measures to provide steam rams for defense against ironclad vessels in western waters.[9]

To see that Ellet's motive and Stanton's purpose were realized one needs only to study the engagements of the Ram Fleet. At Memphis and Vicksburg it did memorable work, but more noteworthy was its engagement up the Yazoo River where David G. Farragut and Grant profited as a result.[10]

When the North proclaimed the blockade of the southern ports, ironclad vessels had not as yet made their appearance in the Navy. It was not until 3 August 1861, that Congress made provision for the investigation and construction of iron-clad steamships or steam-batteries.[11] As a result of this act, three ironclad vessels were recommended to be built. Seventeen proposals were submitted to the board appointed by the Secretary of the Navy. Of these only three were accepted, those of John Ericsson, New York; Merrick & Sons, Philadelphia; and C.S. Bushnell & Co., New Haven, Connecticut.

Ericsson, as is commonly known, built the *Monitor*, which won that ever famous engagement with the *Merrimac* [C.S.S. Virginia] in Hampton Roads, on 9 March 1862. This resulted in an increased number of orders for ironclads. Almost immediately after the contest, the government issued orders for 10 Monitor-type batteries.[12]

Pittsburgh also profited indirectly by the Monitor-Merrimac engagement. A contract was awarded to Mason and Snowden in 1861 for the construction of a Monitor-type boat. The specifications were somewhat different from those under which Ericsson worked. This boat which was christened the *Manayunk*, was not launched until 18 December 1864. The cost was approximately $583,000.[13]

Though only a third class monitor, it was nevertheless four times the size of the original *Monitor*, being 224 feet long, 33 feet wide and drawing 14 feet with a ton-nage of 1,034.[14] In referring to this vessel, George H. Thurston, author of *Pittsburgh and Allegheny in the Centennial Year* says that it "was pronounced by good naval authority as a most admirable boat, in all respects safe to sail around the world."[15]

Another boat of the same type which was also built by Mason and Snowden was the *Umpqua*. It was contracted for in 1863 and completed in September 1866 at a cost of $595,652.66.[16] Being intended for river service, it was somewhat lighter than its mate, the *Manayunk*. Its revolving turret — commonly known as "Cheese Box," was nine feet high and 20 feet in diameter, being armed with an "eleven inch gun and one 150 pounder." On the other hand the turret of the *Manayunk* was 21 feet inside and somewhat stronger armed with two 15-inch guns.[17]

In addition to these two monitors, two other smaller ironclads were built during the Civil War by Pittsburgh firms. Hartupee and Tomlinson was the fortunate firm in this case. The contract was awarded to them in 1862 although the boats were not launched until January 1865. These monitors were named the *Marietta* and *Sandusky* and were produced at a cost of $470,179.14.[18]

The production cost of these war vessels may seem trivial if viewed by present day standards, but two things must be taken into consideration: first, that the iron-ship was then in its infancy, and second, that the super-dreadnaught was not even a dream. Nor was Pittsburgh's naval energy entirely devoted to the building of ironclads, for in the field of deck plating and iron armor its position was prominent. Bailey, Brown and Company produced half the iron plate for the *Kensington*, a million-dollar ironclad under construction at Philadelphia in the year 1862.[19]

Two other million-dollar ironclads, the *Meantonomah*, and *Tonawanda*, were covered with Pittsburgh armor plate. The former was built in New York by the Novelty Iron Works and the latter in Philadelphia by the firm of Merrick and Sons.[20] The plating for these vessels was furnished by the firm of M.K. Moorehead and G.F. McClave at a cost of $222,000.40.[21]

Pittsburgh also furnished one half of the armor plate for the *Ironsides*, an $800,000 vessel, under construction at Philadelphia.[22] On this subject the *Gazette* says: "It may not be generally known that the immense iron plate for the new iron-plated steamships now being built at Philadelphia by Messrs. Merrick & Son. for the government, are being manufactured in this city at the works of Messrs. Bailey, Brown & Co. The plates are 15 feet long, 28-1/2 and 30-1/2 inches wide and four inches thick."[23] Newspapers of Pennsylvania at that time made frequent note of the fact that Pittsburgh forges could turn out sufficient armor plates to cover every vessel in the navy.

Prior to the construction of Ericsson's *Monitor*, the officials of the Navy Department doubted the ability of American foundries to produce plating of the 4-1/2 inch thickness. However true the basis for their statements may have been, later facts did not support their contention. So great was the demand for iron plate that during the year 1863, in Pittsburgh alone, many rolling mills were constructed.

Among these were Messrs. Lyon & Shorb, The Messrs. McKnight and Messrs. Reese, Graff and Dull. The newly constructed mill of the Messrs. McKnight had a capacity of 50 tons of armor plate per week, while Messrs. Reese, Graff and Dull's plate mill had a capacity of 100 tons per week. The plate mills were constructed for the purpose of rolling armor plate for naval use, 10 feet long, one to one and a half inches thick, and weighing from 1,600 pounds to a ton each.[24]

Pittsburgh's industrial ingenuity and energy did not limit itself to naval construction but made a more enviable record in the manufacture of immense engines of war. In the ordnance department, Pittsburgh's position is especially prominent. For these facts it is best to state the history of the Fort Pitt Foundry.

This industrial plant was established in 1803 and continued in existence until about 1870. It was originally located at the corner of Fifth Avenue and Smithfield Street where the Park Building now stands. During the Civil War it was located at Twenty-eighth Street in Allegheny. [All extant sources indicate that during the Civil War, the foundry was actually located in Bayardstown (present-day Strip District) between O'Hara (Twelfth) Street and Walnut (Thirteenth) Street along the Allegheny River.]

The Fort Pitt Foundry supplied the government with ordnance for three wars: the War of 1812, the Mexican War, and the Civil War. Even Oliver Hazard Perry's famous victory on Lake Erie was aided materially by the service of Pittsburgh cannon cast at this foundry.[25] However as the Civil War concerns us most, let us turn our attention toward its contributions to the Union forces.

Among the productions of the Fort Pitt Foundry, the big guns must receive primary consideration. The first of these, the *Union* was a 12-inch rifled cannon, weighing 26 tons. It was completed in the latter part of May 1861 and shipped on 31 May,[26] destined for Fort McHenry in Baltimore Harbor. On reaching its destination it was favorably tested, much to the dismay of the troublesome Baltimoreans. A correspondent who was an eyewitness of the official test wrote: "Some idea of the range of this immense missile may be formed from the fact that it fired the huge ball, weighing five hundred pounds, six miles. The effect was tremendous — shells were thrown through the long sand bank; the force of the firing shook the ground as no other gun has ever done before."[27] At the time this was considered the largest cannon in the world.[28]

Though a subject of much comment at the time, many guns similar to the *Union* were turned out during the period of the war. In all, the Fort Pitt Foundry furnished 1,193 guns, during the period ending 30 June 1865. This lot included eight-, 10- and 12-inch siege mortars, four and a half-inch rifled cannon, eight- and 10-inch howitzers, and eight-, 10-, 12-, 15-inch Columbiads and 20-inch "Rodmans."

The total value of these contributions was approximately $1,600.[29] [Columbiads, which combined the features of the gun, mortar, and howitzer, were large, long-range guns used for seacoast defenses in the 19th century. The term "Rodman" referred to guns manufactured using the Rodman process – a process invented by Thomas J. Rodman that entailed using running water to cool cannons from a hollow core, rather than externally, thereby increasing the durability of the metal. The process facilitated the creation of the largest cannons yet created. The first gun fabricated using the Rodman process was made at the Fort Pitt Foundry in the 1850s].

We are prone to underestimate the value and number of guns, if no comparison is made with the total purchased at that time. For the entire period of the war, the United States government purchased 7,731 cannons, mortars, and columbiads.[30] In other words the Fort Pitt Foundry alone furnished fifteen percent of the entire amount of large ordnance purchased by the government for use in the Civil War.

Among the ordnance furnished by the Fort Pitt Foundry were 73, 15-inch Rodmans, the price of which was $485,500. This again may seem insignificant to us, who are accustomed to billion dollar appropriations, but let us not forget that only eight 15-inch guns were purchased elsewhere, which clearly shows that the Fort Pitt furnished 80 percent of these big guns.[31]

At this point it would not be inappropriate to observe the position held by the Fort Pitt Foundry, both at home and at Washington. From the above data it is evident that there is much truth in the statement made by the *Gazette*, commenting upon the outbreak of a fire there: "It is here that all the big guns are cast for the government and the destruction of these works would be almost as disastrous as the loss of a battle."[32]

In his report for 1863, H.A. Wise, Chief of the Bureau of Ordnance says: "The Fort Pitt Foundry, with its immense facilities and very great experience in the art of founding cannon, was at first the only establishment willing and able to undertake the task of making the 15 inch gun!"[33]

The Confederates had as their main support in the manufacture of guns, the Tredegar Iron Works in Richmond. Its capacity was only two Dahlgren guns per week; this was greatly surpassed by that of the Fort Pitt Foundry, which produced 12 guns of the largest caliber per week.[34]

A product which excited much comment was the famous 20-inch Rodman gun. The first one, as would naturally be expected, was cast at the Fort Pitt Foundry on 12 February 1864, at a cost of $32,000.[35] It was cast in the presence of many distinguished men, including Major Rodman, the inventor of the principle. The *Gazette* described the casting as "one of the greatest feats in iron founding yet achieved."

In ascertaining the facts in the greatest feat in iron founding yet achieved, it is seen that 80 tons of molten metal were required. The gun was cast hollow, and the core was kept cool by a constant stream of cold water passing through it. In the finished state it weighed 56 tons, being 20 feet long over all, (the bore being 18-feet long.) The maximum diameter was 64 inches, minimum, 34 inches. It fired a 1,000 [1,080] pound [solid iron] ball [or] a 750-pound [hollow] shell, charged with 100 pounds of powder. This gun was also at its time the largest gun in the world; with the exception of the stone throwing bronze gun at the Dardanelles.[36]

This gun had a great moral effect upon the enemy. It seemed, however, that those firing the gun were in greater danger than those fired upon. This was due no doubt to the imperfect and somewhat primitive method of casting. That this is true can be inferred from the fact that very few such guns were cast. [Actually, no guns cast using the Rodman system are known to have burst. This cannot be said of the earlier cast iron Columbiads. The expense and weight of Rodman guns is what limited their production.]

The first order for shells purchased in this district by the government also came from Fort Pitt, and consisted of 440 eight-inch shot and 812 eight-inch columbiad shells.[37] The first contract for projectiles was also made with the Fort Pitt Foundry on 25 April 1866, for 1000, eight- inch balls of reduced caliber.[38]

From 9 April 1861, to the end of the fiscal year 30 June 1863, the Fort Pitt Foundry furnished 33,071 cannon balls, shells and other projectiles valued at something like $100,000. But the record for the production of the greatest number for the period belongs to Smith, Park & Co., who furnished 196,320 projectiles valued at $92,000. Among the firms which furnished projectiles were Anderson & Phillips, Pennock, Hart & Co., and J.C. Bidwell of the Pittsburgh Plow Works. These collectively furnished 29,537 projectiles valued at $103,085.[39] These figures, large as they are, however, do not mean much to us until we discover that they represent 10 percent of all projectiles purchased by the Government during the period from the beginning of the Rebellion to 30 June 1863.[40]

From 30 June 1863 to 30 June 1865, the Fort Pitt Foundry has the record for the largest number of projectiles. For this period it sold to the Government 161,000 projectiles at a cost of $104,719. Smith, Park & Co. sold during the same period 110,645 projectiles at a price of $88,721. Pennock & Totten furnished 5,527 projectiles at a cost of $7,636. Joseph Pennock furnished 28,260 projectiles at a cost of $61,526.[41] On consulting the *House Executive Documents* it is seen that during this final two-year period the Pittsburgh firms again furnished 10 percent of all projectiles purchased by the government.[42]

The Fort Pitt Foundry is a subject of both pride and value to Pittsburgh. As has been stated before in this paper, it contributed greatly to our government in surmounting the difficulties of the various wars, and its last service was in helping to save the Union.

Further enlargement is necessary before the full force of this view is realized. From available records it has been found that the Fort Pitt Foundry furnished more ordnance than any other firm with the exception of the Colt Patent Firearms Company, Hartford, Connecticut and Robert P. Parrott, Cold Spring, New York. Among the strong competitors were E. Remington & Son of Ilion, New York, Savage Arms Company, of Middleton, Connecticut, and Sharps Rifle Arms Company, of Hartford, Connecticut.[43] The sad part connected with this is that the Fort Pitt Foundry left no successors in the firearms field while its competitors are today internationally known.

Pittsburgh did its part in providing comfort for the Union boys by furnishing 19,778 blankets and 37,893 articles of clothing as well as 674 tents for the first of the war.[44] From the *Pittsburgh Evening Chronicle* of 11 September 1861, we glean this item, "Four thousand sets of harness have been contracted here. Each set will harness a four mule team. About two thousand sets are now ready for delivery and the balance will be put through with the least possible delay."

It is to be regretted and lamented that records on this subject are sadly inadequate and have for the most part been destroyed as "useless documents." However, in the *Rebellion Record of Allegheny County*, we find that "No provision having been made either in this city or Harrisburg, by the authorities, in 1861, for uniforming the three-month volunteers, the men demurred from going until they were suitably clothed. B.F. Jones, Esq., assumed the task of equipping one company and depositing his check for $3,000 ordered the clothing to be furnished, and set about collecting the amount to reimburse himself. Over $13,000 were collected in a day or two, and with this ten companies were uniformed."[45] The material furnished consisted of uniforms, undergarments, overcoats, caps and blankets, and was furnished by the following firms: Morganstern and Brother, Louis Kiehnieson, J.M. Little, J.C. Watt, A Frowenfield and Brother, and C.H. Paulson. Two of the companies outfitted included the Duquesne Greys and Washington Infantry.

In addition to this local contribution, Pittsburgh firms supplied the Government with 871 wagons furnished for the most part by Phelps, Parke & Company, and Mr. Aeschelman,[46] and the *Gazette* of 12 September 1861, says, "We learn that Mr. J.C. Bidwell, proprietor of the Pittsburgh Plow Works has received a contract from the government for the construction of fifty-four heavy gun-carriages."

Pittsburgh's splendid relief work, which unfortunately is not in the province of this paper, was aided indirectly, by the manufacture of thirty-five ambulances which were supplied to the government.

To keep the fires of industry burning, approximately 5,500,000 tons of the famous Pittsburgh coal were mined during the Civil War. This was 423,000 tons more than for any preceding period of similar duration.[47] To transport the Civil War tonnage of coal in this district would require seventy-five miles of barges.

Though only a dim perspective of the industrial contribution of Pittsburgh has been obtained, this paper shows that Pittsburgh with a population of only about 50,000[48] contributed largely to the success of the Northern cause. Further, that there was great sincerity and unity of purpose among its citizens in their enthusiastic support of this cause. ★

CHAPTER 7

THE SANITARY FAIR

BY DOROTHY DANIEL

Women played an important, though often-overlooked, role in Western Pennsylvania's contribution to the Union war effort. Young Irish women, for example, constituted the majority of the workforce in the cartridge-making division of Pittsburgh's Allegheny Arsenal. Others served as vivandières – women unofficially attached to regiments for the purpose of performing camp maintenance and nursing duties. In this article, Dorothy Daniel discusses one of the most significant accomplishments of women on the Western Pennsylvania home front — their involvement in the Pittsburgh Sanitary Fair of 1864. Modeled after similar events in other American cities and carried out under the auspices of the United States Sanitary Commission, the Pittsburgh Sanitary Fair was a grassroots attempt to care for sick and wounded soldiers by raising money to resupply medical stockpiles in army camps and hospitals. Pittsburgh women played a leading role in making the event a success. This essay first appeared in the Summer 1958 issue of *Western Pennsylvania Historical Magazine*.

Left: Pittsburgh's Sanitary Fair, June 1864. — Carnegie Library of Pittsburgh, Pittsburgh Photographic Library

P ITTSBURGH'S SANITARY FAIR WAS NOT THE FIRST OF ITS KIND, NOR THE last, nor the greatest, nor the one to receive the most national publicity. Pittsburgh's Sanitary Fair, it must be acknowledged, seemed a trifle homespun when compared to the Great Central Fair in Philadelphia. No "large volume of nearly six hundred pages" remains to record the glories of our efforts in behalf of the United States Sanitary Commission in 1864 as may be found in Cincinnati reporting the wonders of the Great Western Sanitary Fair. But when all the quarters and dimes had been counted and all the costs deducted, Pittsburgh's donation to the cause was $3.47 per capita. In this we were first. No other community gave so much.

Sharp-penned critics "allowed as how" Pittsburgh could afford to give generously since she had grown fat on munitions ordered for the Armies of the North. Less prejudiced observers noticed that the bulk of contributions to Pittsburgh's "San'tary Fair" came from women and children, farmers, miners, grocers, saddlers, teachers, ministers, artists, musicians, and others keenly motivated by a desire to alleviate suffering.[1]

Our Sanitary Fair was unique as Pittsburgh is unique. It followed the general pattern suggested by a Mrs. Jane Hoge who started the whole fair benefit idea in Chicago in January 1864. Under the leadership of Felix R. Brunot, the Pittsburgh Sanitary Fair became a community enterprise, the benefits of which left their mark on charitable endeavors hereabouts from that day to this.

At first the do-it-yourself methods of Mr. Brunot and his committees were ridiculed by more sophisticated entrepreneurs as amateurish and bungling. When the general committee reported net receipts of $322,217.98 — which is a great deal of money to raise in 18 days in any decade — nothing more was said of method, emphasis swinging happily to accomplishment.

"Sanitary" as a word, meant something more in 1864 than the more or less limited non-microbious connotation of today. Its first meaning "relating to the preservation of health" had been useful in describing the astounding loss of life among the British troops during the Crimean war. As a result of epidemics, more than half the British soldiers in the field would never go home again.

At the beginning of the Civil War it became starkly plain to the Medical Corps of the Army of the Potomac that caring for a small national army in peace times was not the same problem either in application or scope as administering to the needs of hundreds of thousands of inadequately equipped volunteers. The Honorable Simon Cameron, who was then the heartily unpopular Secretary of War but a Pennsylvanian withal, at the suggestion of the medical bureau at Washington appointed the United States Sanitary Commission on the ninth day of June 1861.

In his orders Secretary Cameron directed that the Sanitary Commission "direct its inquiries to the principles and practices connected with the inspection of recruits and enlisted men; to the sanitary condition of the volunteers; to the means of preserving and restoring the health, and of securing the general comfort and efficiency of the troops; to the proper provisions for cooks, nurses and hospitals; and to other subjects of like nature."

The United States Sanitary Commission became a volunteer organization with offices in the Treasury Building in Washington. It was committed to cooperation with the army medical staff but independent of it. Mr. George T. Strong of 68 Wall Street, New York, became the treasurer of the commission and the first big-scale, all-out, community-level, health-betterment, fundraising campaign began.

It was generally understood that the Sanitary Commission did not want government funds because such subsidy would make them prey to political patronage and control. A government agency that was self-supporting was a novelty. Its fine humanitarian purposes and its high ethical code of financing and administration appealed to the hearts of those mothers, sisters, aunts, cousins and grandmothers left behind. The men folk, fathers and the like served on committees and helped to organize the events, fetched and carried, climbed the ladders and paid the bills. Even so, the Sanitary Fairs of 1864 were generally conceded to be accomplishments of the women folk.

It is easier to declare independence than to sustain it, and support for the commission had been spotty and disappointing. The whole amount collected by the treasurer of the Sanitary Commission from its organization in 1861 until October 1863 was a little over $800,000. Of this, $500,000 had come from California. Costs of the Sanitary Commission were running almost double the income.

Lotteries, auctions, and cotillions had been sponsored by the various committees of the Sanitary Commission but, as willing as the people were to contribute, nothing seemed to bring substantial results until Mrs. Hoge of Chicago got her committee together and set up a bazaar in Bryan Hall on Clark Street, opposite the courthouse.

> Mrs. Hoge's fair was little more than a glorified church bazaar. Every variety of fancy and useful article was for sale on the main floor. The lower part of Bryan Hall was turned into an immense dining room, where hot dinners were served daily to 1,500 people. Mrs. Hoge and Mrs. Livermore were the managers of the great undertaking which continued for two weeks with evening entertainments, the exhibition of rare relics and trophies and everything that could be arranged to give variety to the program.[2]

Mrs. Hoge's Sanitary Fair was an immediate success and representatives from the executive committee of the Woman's Pennsylvania Branch of the Commission went out to Chicago to see how it was done. Pittsburgh's representatives were Miss Rachel W. M'Fadden and Mrs. Felix R. Brunot. They studied the Chicago technique and then returned to announce to Mr. Brunot that Pittsburgh should have such a fair, only one that would be much better.

Mr. Brunot talked with Thomas Bakewell about it. Everyone talked to Thomas Bakewell about everything. He was, next to the venerable Judge William Wilkins, Pittsburgh's most distinguished and civic-minded citizen. Moreover he had been appointed, early in the war, President of the Pittsburgh Sanitary Committee, a branch or local chapter of the larger United States Sanitary Commission in Washington. Felix Brunot was first vice president of the committee. R. Miller, Jr. was second vice president, J.R. Hunter, secretary, and James Park, Jr., Treasurer. The "Ladies' Branch" of the Sanitary Committee was organized with Miss Rachel M'Fadden, President, Miss Anna Jackson and Miss Mary L. Jackson, Secretaries, and Miss Martha P. Bakewell, Treasurer.

The committee met and listened to Miss M'Fadden's report of Mrs. Hoge's Chicago bazaar. For Pittsburgh to undertake such a fair on an equal scale of grandeur seemed pretentiously ambitious but Mr. Brunot and some of the others felt sure that if money was ever to be raised for the Sanitary Commission some means must be found of generating unusual generosity and at the same time converting the gifts of food and merchandise into cash on the local thresholds of these charities.

Thereupon it was moved and seconded that such a fair take place in June of 1864 and that Mr. Felix R. Brunot be the General Chairman of the same. Mr. W.S. Haven volunteered his services as printer and his first assignment was to issue the "Address" which was the 1864 equivalent of a general announcement.

ADDRESS

The Pittsburgh Sanitary Committee, a branch of the U.S. Sanitary Commission, established for the relief of the sick and wounded soldiers, announce to the public that a Great Fair will be held at Pittsburgh, Pa., commencing on such day as the Executive Committee will hereafter make known.

The object of the Fair is to obtain money to enable the Sanitary Commission to proceed with their good work with increased energy and usefulness. The practical workings of the United States Sanitary Commission have been of such incalculable good, and have met such high approval from the entire people, that an enumeration of its claims is useless.

Every one feels it a duty to succor the wounded, sick and disabled soldier. The promptings of every loyal heart speak clearly, that we, who do not bear the dint and turmoil of the battle, should provide liberally for the 'war-worn sons of the Republic'. Christian charity speaks trumpet-tongued to each and every one, telling us to tender to the wants of those who are sick, wounded and disabled in our country's glorious cause.

The duties of our common humanity teach us that all should unite in the cause; and if a cup of cold water is not to go unrewarded, what immortal favors will not be bestowed on those who are the liberal donors to so deserving and charitable a work.

This is not merely local matter. We cordially invite the donations, contributions, aid and co-operation, not only of Allegheny City, Birmingham, Allegheny County and the State of Pennsylvania, but of Ohio, and all the States of the Republic. The recipients of the care of the Sanitary Commission are the soldiers of the United States, without regard to what special State enlisted from, citizens or foreigners, old or young and without respect to sect, creed, faith or color. All who fight and are disabled in the cause of our common country, are embraced in the management and care of the United States Sanitary Commission. We therefore ask the hearty co-operation and aid of all.

Donations of money will be thankfully received by the Honorary Treasurer of the Fair, N. Holmes, Esq.

Contributions of merchandise of every nature will be received by the Committees appointed for that purpose.

The Fair will be under the control of the Executive Committee, F.R. Brunot, Esq,
Chairman, and replies will meet prompt attention addressed to
S.F. VON BONNHORST, Esq.
Honorary Corresponding Secretary Pittsburgh U.S.
Sanitary Commission Fair, Pittsburgh Pa.

Executive Committee
Miss Rachel W. M'Fadden, President   Felix R. Brunot, Chairman

Mrs. Felix R. Brunot   Jno. H. Shoenberger
Mrs. Tieran   Thos. M. Howe
Mrs. Paxton   J.I. Bennett
Mrs. Price   John W. Chalfant
Mrs. Wm. Bakewell   Chas. W. Batchelor
Mrs. Kay   B.F. Jones
Mrs. Jno. Watt   James O'Connor
Mrs. Brady Wilkins   James Park, Jr.
Mrs. Algernon Bell   Mark W. Watson
Miss Susan Sellers   Jno. Watt
Miss Mary Moorhead   W.S. Haven
Miss Ella Stewart, Honorary Secretary
Mrs. M'Millan, Assistant Secretary
Miss Bakewell, Assistant Secretary
W.D. M'Gowan, Secretary[3]

Headquarters and offices were established at 96 Water Street, with J.E. Brady, Jr.
as Secretary and the work of organizing committees began at once. In March,
Mr. Brady was still trying to conquer the mountain of work before him in longhand.
Even with volunteers from the women's committee, the work became arduous since
it was considered important that each committee appointment be specific:

Rooms of the Executive Committee
Pittsburgh Sanitary Fair.
21st March 1864
Hon. James Veech.
Dear Sir:
    The executive committee, Pittsburgh Sanitary Fair have appointed you a member
of the Foreign Corresponding Committee. A meeting of the Committee was held at the
rooms of the Sanitary Fair on Saturday 19th March at 3 p.m. when the following
business was transacted.

On motion the following division of labors of the Committee was made.

To address Generals, Official Personages of U.S. Prominent Statesmen, Merchants and so forth: Hon. W.F. Johnston and James O'Connor, Esquire.

To address Judges of the Courts, Eminent Lawyers Jurists and so forth: Hon. Judge Williams and Hon. Jas.Veech

To address Governors of States and State Officials: Hon. E.H. Stowe.

To address Poets, Literary men, Authors and men of Science: Rev. W.A. Passavant and Prof. Barker.

To address distinguished Catholic Ecclesiastics of Europe and U.S.: Right Revd. Bishop Domenec.

To address distinguished Protestant Divines of Europe and U.S.: Revd. Dr. Jacobus.

Prof. Barker asked if the intention of addressing letters (as above classified was 1st to obtain autographic replies to be sold for benefit Sanitary Fair. 2: to obtain an expression of sympathy for the Cause and 3: to obtain (if possible) donations of money from the persons addressed and in reply it was stated that such were the purposes and intentions of the Committee.

On motion it was resolved that all manuscripts be carefully engrossed by Mr. J.E. Brady, Jr. and after being signed by all of the members Foreign Corresponding Committee be forwarded to the parties to whom they are addressed. On motion immediate action was resolved on and the Secy. requested to advise all the members of The Committee. On motion adjourned to meet Tuesday 29th March at 3 P.M. at rooms Sanitary Committee. Hoping you will bear the meeting in mind and that all your energies and sympathies may be enlisted in the Cause so that we may make the Foreign Correspondence one of the most interesting departments of the Fair.

I am very respectfully yours,

J.E. Brady, Jr. Sec'y.[4]

Committee appointments began to pile up and it was discovered that for the good of all many individuals served with equal effectiveness on several committees. James Veech, for instance, was an author, a lawyer, an historian, an art collector, and a mature man who was easy to get along with, yet one who could be counted on to speak his mind, have original ideas, and do more than his share of the work.

Thomas Bakewell had agreed to be chairman of the Private Libraries and Literary Contributions Committee and he asked that James Veech also serve on this committee as one of Pittsburgh's authors. By the time this committee was appointed Mr. Brady had writer's cramp and his volunteers had gone about business setting up the Art Committee and working furiously to assemble the curios for the Old Curiosity Shop. Mr. Haven came to the rescue with a dignified notice printed in script with spaces left for the name of the committee and its proposed member to be filled in by pen. This notice read in part:

The general management and responsibility for success in the Department depend mainly on the exertions of your Committee.

You are requested to secure, if you can, the co-operation and contributions:

1 – Of every person or firm in Western Pennsylvania and Eastern Ohio engaged or in any way interested in the Department allotted to you.

2 – Of all in the chief cities and towns in all parts of the loyal North, or in any Foreign Country, should the latter seem to you practicable or proper.

3 – You are requested to appoint co-operating Committees wherever you may deem it best to do so.

There will be general meetings of all the Committees called from time to time, at which you are requested to attend, or be represented by one of your members, to report progress.

The Head Quarters of the Executive Committee will be at the Rooms of the Iron Association, No. 96 Water street, where the Secretary will be found at all times, and the Chairman or members every afternoon, until the opening of the Fair.

Should you be unwilling, or for any reason unable to serve, please send a written notice to that effect. Hoping to receive such active co-operation from you and your Committee as will insure success in your Department, we are, Very Respectfully, Yours: The Executive Committee.[5]

And so it came about that every man, woman, and child in Pittsburgh and Allegheny City became in some way involved in the Sanitary Fair. This was not the usual method of organization. Other cities had committees, it is true, but no other community could boast of the unconfused and unconfusing organization that contributed to Pittsburgh's success.

Mr. Haven found it necessary, in the absence of telephones, to print up a series of committee meeting announcements and these fluttered like confetti on the desks of bankers, lawyers, industrialists, merchants and the wives and daughters of committee members who were themselves members of committees.

Henry Kleber wrote a "Relief Polka" dedicated to the "Committee of Ladies of the Sanitary Fair"; and Miss Emma K. Ogden, the first woman medical missionary to India, made a flag with 36 stars to fly from the flagstaff above Monitor Hall.[6]

Providentially Allegheny City was in the process of building a new city hall strategically located on the edge of the Common. The upper floors of the new city hall were allocated at once for the Art Gallery, the Old Curiosity Shop, and the Photograph Gallery. Means then had to be found to build the necessary sheds to house the dining room, the industrial and agricultural exhibits.

At this moment of dilemma members of the executive committee learned of an old exhibition building about to be torn down in Cleveland. A volunteer corps of drays, horses, wagons, carpenters, boys who were handy with hammers, men who could sling sledges, and committee members interested in seeing a job well done, left early one morning for the west. The returning expedition looked more like pilgrims setting out to build Solomon's Temple than volunteers with a dining hall in mind. But they were greeted with cheers and encouragement at the Commons and men who couldn't get away from work to drive all the way to Cleveland joined up on the construction work. The resulting buildings had a jaunty, gay, here-today-and-gone-tomorrow look which delighted the people and made them very proud because not one penny of "the funds" had gone into their construction.

There was talk for a while of publishing a daily newspaper on the grounds but this idea was abandoned because the Pittsburgh papers had contributed so generously both in advertising space and editorial content. For weeks before the opening of the Fair, the *Gazette* and the *Post* carried columns of names from the Treasurer's report. Company names were listed under their category of manufacture. The Flint Glass Manufacturers Association contributed as follows:

Bakewell Pears and Company	$500.00
James B. Lyon and Company	$400.00
McKee and Brothers	$250.00
Phillips and Best	$250.00
Bryce Richards and Company	$200.00
E.D. Dithridge	$200.00
Adams and Co.	$200.00
King and Co.	$100.00
Atterbury and Co.	$100.00
T.A. Evans and Co.	$100.00
Shepard and Co.	$50.00
H.S. Hamilton and Co.	$50.00
	$2,400.00

Solicitation was also made to the employees of corporations and foundries and when these lists were turned in to the treasurer they were printed in full in the newspapers. N.G. Bigley's Coal Works had 95 workmen. M.J. Bigley started off the list by giving $1,000. His employees, all of which are listed, gave two and three dollar donations totaling $274.50.

By opening day $84,059.37 had been raised in this way and each name and organization had been printed. Iron City Commercial College gave $500. Mr. Avery's Philomathean Institute gave $75. Captain W. Smith's Tow Boat, the *Bengal Tiger*, gave $100.

While the finance committee and the publicity committee were hard at work, other activity was frantically in progress. The newspapers carried appeals from the various committees of which the Horticultural and Floral Department was most detailed:

> The committee on Plants and Fruits and Flowers confidentially appeal to the aid of all Horticulturists and Florists both Amateur, Commercial and Professional. The laudable object of the Fair and the apparent exigencies of the time, and the development of each day alone, will urge the Patriot and Philanthropist.
>
> We solicit your donations or contributions of such articles as will adorn and render attractive the Department under our charge, which is of ample extent and where careful attendants will always be at hand that the owners of plants may rest assured that their collections will be daily cared for. In addition to the ordinary products of the greenhouse and garden, the Committee also solicits contributions of Bouquets, Baskets of Flowers, Floral Designs, Hanging Baskets, Flower Stands, Fern Casks, Aviaries, Gardening Implements, Native Wine, Garden Seats and Vases, Horticultural Iron Work, Cut Flowers, Dried Flowers, Wax Flowers, Leather Flowers, Phantom Bouquets, Autumn Leaves, Aquaria, Seeds, Gardening Books, Fountains, Horticultural Wire Work, Horticultural China and Glass, Horticultural Pottery, Foreign and Exotic Fruit, Dried Fruit, Wax Fruit and Garden Statuary.
>
> In short, Rustic Ornaments of every kind, or anything of a rural or rustic character that does not strictly belong to the Agricultural Department.
>
> Daily contributions of cut flowers, bouquets, designs, baskets, etc., so as to insure a constant and regular supply during the Fair, will be very acceptable and contributors will please arrange with the chairman of the committee at Floral Hall.
> Wm. S. Bissell, Chairman.[7]

The Old Curiosity Shop made a similar appeal and long before the buildings were ready the exhibits began to arrive. Although the Fair had been announced for the first of June it looked for a time as though nothing would be ready.

The editor of the *Post* observed a little nervously on 30 May, "though the buildings of this Fair are rapidly approaching completion, yet the time for the opening ceremonies is coming as rapidly, and it will require all the exertions of the mechanics employed to have it prepared for the reception of the many contributions now arriving."

The Art Gallery and the Old Curiosity Shop were delayed in getting into their quarters in the New City Hall but since there was little involved but the hanging of pictures they quickly recovered and were photographed opening day with the women's art committee and the participating artists, George Hetzel, Trevor McClurg and William C. Wall.

The bazaar itself was a little more difficult to put together. Under the general direction of Mr. Eaton the newly erected hall presented its problems. "The long range of counters is being covered with white muslin, on which are placed strips of red and blue paper, making the red, white and blue conspicuous. Flags are suspended from every arch and pillar and beautiful wreaths of evergreen from every rafter. The building is furnished [with] an abundance of gas pipes which, when lighted up in the evening will add a peculiar brilliancy to the other decorations."

These evergreen wreaths and braided bands of ground pine and ivy were contributed by volunteers. Notices were issued through the newspapers and the committee that evergreen wreaths and woven strips of decoration would be used. People living in the wooded sections of Westmoreland and Fayette counties brought wagon loads of woven evergreens and yet it was not enough so that a second appeal was made almost at the last minute.[8] Since there was no longer time for weaving the intricate garlands, the committee had to settle for boughs of hemlock, cedar and spruce which made the Bazaar hall smell tantalizingly like Christmas Day in June.

In the south end of Floral Hall stood the Garden of Eden of which the *Gazette* reported: "The gardens are elaborately wrought specimen of rustic scenery. There are trees and rocks, fruit and flowers, sticks and moss, hills and dales, groves and bowers, and indeed everything that could make a place enchanting and lovely. There stands the forbidden tree, around it is coiled the serpent, and near it stands Adam and Eve in matchless innocence." Included in the scene of our ultimate beginnings were two parent pheasants with young, a squirrel on a limb, assorted birds and the nose of a groundhog.

James P. Barr, editor and publisher of the *Daily Post*, was a man of considerable cultural attainments. He liked to do his own reporting of events which interested him and his editorial criticisms of concerts, recitals and theatricals are classic commentaries on his contemporaries and their way of life. His preview of the Fair is typically leisurely:

One of the most unique and peculiar constructions is the "Union College" for children. This little building is not more than ten feet square, built in true cottage style, and finished with beautiful and expensive cornice. Attached to it will be a little garden about ten feet square, around which will be an iron railing fence, and in the center of which will be a beautiful fountain, throwing up continual jets of water which will fall again in a basin below. In the garden will be a variety of choice flowers. The "Union College" is designed and superintended by Mrs. Bell.

At the west end of the Bazaar is a beautiful gallery or platform, erected for the accommodation of musicians. This place has regular stairways and is finished in good style.

Another object of special attraction is the Scotch Booth on the south side of the Bazaar which is built in true rustic style and thatched with straw.

There are many other stands variously decorated with different kinds of tinseling, red paper, with silver leaves and golden vines.

To describe Floral hall is a task for which our pen is inadequate. The peculiarities of almost every nation, will here be represented in grotesque and appropriate scenery. There will be the German Grotto near the Rhine by which a river or stream representing a river will flow during the continuance of the Fair. The buildings of English, Scotch, Irish, French, Swiss, Chinese and almost every other nation will have a representative here in miniature size and characteristic style.

Monitor Hall was the largest of the buildings constructed for the Fair and the ugliest. It stands out as the building with the tower in photographs of the Fair. It was also the most popular of all exhibits with boys and their fathers for reasons Mr. Barr previews:

In Monitor Hall is already a pattern of the mammoth guns cast at the Fort Pitt Works and specimen of cannon ball and bombshell. Small ordnance and mortars are also represented here. And then the canal on which will proudly ride the little gunboat or Monitor and other curious and attractive sights can be witnessed here.

Audience Hall is not yet completed. The workmen are just nailing down the seats. They will consist of four rows or tiers, thirty in each row making in all one hundred and twenty seats. Each seat will hold twelve persons at least — perhaps sixteen. Then there is a large space between those seats and the platform so that the hall will have capacity for a great number of patrons. On the outside or out-end, eastward is a kind of portico or raised platform which will hold about twenty musicians.

Mr. Barr sadly related that Mechanics Hall was not ready yet, with only two days to go, but despite his gloomy apprehensions, by noon the first day of June the committee in charge declared the Fair officially open ready or not.

The day had dawned with a misty, muggy red sun rising over Grant's hill and the worst was feared for the procession. The air was tingling with a high state of excitement. Farmers began to arrive early with donations for the dining hall and their teams of horses and lines of wagons stretched all the way down the river road as far as General Robinson's back gate so that no one could find a place to hitch to.

Notice had appeared in the papers for the Vigilant Steam Fire Company to meet at the Engine House at two o'clock P.M. fully equipped to be ready to march. The "Boiler's Union" had apparently misunderstood the general orders or else wanted to get there first with the loudest. Just as everyone else was assembling the Boiler's Union lined up in front of their hall at the corner of Smithfield and Fifth Avenue and then, preceded by a brass band of their own, started out toward Wood Street and thence to the fair grounds marching and singing away to beat all. Somebody shooed them back up toward the Monongahela House and there they had to wait, sweating out their shirts and damping their thirsts at the Mechanic's Pub, until 4:30 when the procession finally began.

The mayors of both cities, Pittsburgh and Allegheny, had issued proclamations suspending all kinds of employment from three o'clock to seven o'clock so that the streets were lined with people from Water Street, where the procession was forming, to the very gates of the Fair. This delayed the event somewhat as did the marshals who found themselves overwhelmed by a number of fire companies who had arrived with their engines polished to participate without either an invitation or a previously-announced intention. The longer the delay the more the marchers seemed to disappear into thin air. At last it was decided to start out with the West Chester Cadets and Band who were still in order, and let the fire company units and the Boiler's Union catch up the best they could.

At 4:30 P.M. on 1 June, under a cloudy but clearing sky, the procession moved away from the Monongahela House, bands blaring, thousands cheering, the Governor of Pennsylvania, the officers of the Fair, the mayors and the councils followed by Smith's Brass Band splitting ears and lifting hearts as nothing in the whole wide world but a brass band can do.

There were nine engine companies as it turned out: The Eagle, Allegheny, Duquesne, Neptune, Hope, Good Intent, General Grant, Relief, and the Vigilant. After the fire engines and their companies came more bands and that part of the Boiler's Union still of a mind to march, followed by citizens. When they got to the Fair Grounds in Allegheny City the Governor, officers and their party went immediately to Audience Hall. Here the ceremonies were to take place.

Unhappily for the record, no member of the press found admittance. It was with greatest difficulty that Governor Curtin was squeezed into the hall among the 2,000 people filling the area designed for little more than half that number. Reporters, editors, and very important persons stood helplessly outside with the other 20,000 first-dayers. And the Governor's well chosen words are lost to the ages.

Mr. Barr took a dim view of the apparent success:

The editor was reckoning without the West-Chester cadets whom Felix Brunot had with remarkable foresight invited to camp on the Commons for the 18 days of the Fair. These young men of "good" families were a kind of honor guard for the governor. They wore handsomely tailored uniforms, singularly of gray color, and they marched with precision and dignity. There were 120 in the cadet corps and they added their own attraction to the exhibits at the fair, particularly for the young ladies.

The Dining Hall was one of the chief attractions at the fair and one requiring a high degree of organization. The supplies for the dinners were donations from farmers and others in the district who were unable to give cash to the cause or who found in their surplus meat, vegetables or fruit to share with the committee. Mrs. B.F. Jones was in general charge of the dining room and Mrs. Samuel McClung supervised the kitchen. The ladies had a basic menu which they endeavored to follow from day to day but they could never be sure when they arrived at the fair at six o'clock in the morning, just what would have been left on their doorstep during the night. Meals were served family style. The members of the committee waited on the tables, peeled the potatoes, set the tables and prepared vegetables. The actual cooking was done by professional cooks whose services were donated by their employers.

Many of the tables in the large dining room had banners above them: Butler, Washington, Uniontown, Greensburg, Etna, and Wilkinsburg, so that visitors from those towns might eat together. Another novelty of the dining room was the confection Pagoda in the center of the room where candy was sold at all times. The daughters of the committee prepared homemade candy and brought it to the Pagoda where it sold almost as soon as it arrived.

Mechanics Hall was popular because of the variety of its modern inventions and home improvements:

In passing around we noticed card frames of a peculiar structure, spring mattresses; patent desks; magnificent stair rods carved and ornamental glassware; circular saws; all kinds of patent pumps, one of which is doubled geared and is propelled by a crank throwing a continuous and beautiful stream of water. There are also near these pumps patent shower baths of a novel construction. Then there are apartments of trunks, whips, saddles, leather, saw plates, brass kettles, the most exquisitely finished cutlery and hardware; gold plated sword sheaths, an iron plate from the Sligo Works one hundred inches in diameter; washing machines of every description; samples of flour in the sack, cooper's barrels and kegs; grain drills, hay rakes, and reaping machines of different patterns, farmer's portable grist mills, patent cider and grape mills, the best specimens of chewing tobacco, and a thousand other curiosities that may have escaped our notice.[10]

Nor was this all. In the Old Curiosity Shop were other wonders:

a conical shaped steel pointed cannon ball that had been captured at Fort Donaldson [sic]; a military trophy captured at Falling Water; fans contributed by rebel prisoners, a large chain the links of which were made out of one block of solid iron; an Indian pipe that belonged to the chief of the Creek Indians; swords that had been at different times presented to Brigadier General Alexander Hays; Bibles one hundred years old; a printed public notice of the first grant of lands in Pennsylvania to planters in America; specimens of Continental money; autograph of Robert Fulton; a Chinese hat; table upon which the Declaration of Independence was written; the chair in which John Hancock sat when he presided at the meeting of Delegates that framed and signed that instrument; Indian beads; dress worn by Queen Victoria at her coronation; image of the Virgin Mary cast in Rome one thousand years ago; a Mexican hat; a Rebel Jewel-case; General Washington's piano…. These form but a small portion of curiosities to be seen in the Old Curiosity Shop, but they may serve as a kind of index which will point out the peculiarities of the things to be seen there.[11]

One would think that everything from kitchen to curiosity shop going so much better than had been anticipated, folks would have been as merry as a wedding bell, but such was not the case. Although the cause was humanitarian, the committees were human.

The first big and public problem arose because of David Blythe. Back some months before when they were tearing down the Old City Hall in order to make way for the New City Hall, the town council of Allegheny City decided to have a picture taken of the building, and it was further decided that each member of the governing body should stick his head out of a window. The picture resulting caused no little comment, some bordering on the ribald.

When it came time to take a picture of the Sanitary Fair procession, the committee decided to commission the artist David Blythe (his prices being less than those of other local artists) to do a sketch and then a painting of the procession, the committee, Governor Andrew Curtin and the West-Chester cadets.

Unfortunately Blythe had friends among the members of the fire engine companies and the Boiler's Union and during the hour and a half wait for the festivities to begin, the artist joined his more mechanically minded friends at the bar. While some of the firemen and a few of the union members managed to catch up with the parade, poor Blythe never made it.

Several days later, reprimanded by the officers, he determined to make amends. So he painted a picture of a parade as he envisioned it with the Democrats, staid Presbyterians that they were, taking the place of the bibulous members of the Boiler's Union. So deft was Blythe and so devastating his art there was not the faintest shadow of a doubt which gentlemen were thus included in the mass portrait of a parade.

It is doubtful whether Felix Brunot saw Blythe's painting before it was hung in the Art Gallery. Blythe was already represented by "The School Master" and "Robert Burns," but because Mr. Brunot was both general chairman and a Republican he was suspect. Our friend Mr. Barr was first to call attention to the painting in the columns of the *Post*. Mr. Blythe replied in the *Gazette*. Feelings flared and then to add to it someone walked off with a life-sized portrait of General George McClellan from the East Liberty booth and there were accusations of factionalism of the worst kind.

David Blythe's letter published in the *Gazette* on 14 June, did, as it was intended to do, sprinkle salt on the open wounds of Democratic dignity. "I never thought of the difficulties which — lay in the way, but was led along simply by the idea that modern Democracy, to be truthfully represented, must exhibit three fold compound, viz: 'washed, unwashed, and unterrified.' To reach these points of excellency with the pencil I know of no way, but to adopt the 'representative principal' one which the *Post* as yet has not denied me."

Poor Mr. Brunot was catching it from all sides. His brother-in-law, George Hogg, had been raising Cashmere goats on his farm near Brownsville and he persuaded Brunot to build a pen for 12 of the creatures at the end of the Audience Hall for display and possible encouragement in the breeding of goats. Rumor had it that Hogg had paid a thousand dollars a head for his original stock and this in itself made his goats something of a curiosity. Normally the most docile of creatures, the thundering of oratory, the crashing of brass bands and the fluted notes of the local sopranos stimulated the animals to the exercise of talents long dormant. Such bleating and baaing had never been heard west of the Alleghenies. The daytime performances were after a time discontinued, the goats giving ground after nightfall.

In spite of General McClellan, David Blythe, the Boiler's Union and the Cashmere goats, and a hundred other incidents that really only served to brighten the excitement, Pittsburgh's Sanitary Fair was an outstanding success. It was a busy 18 days that left the committees gasping with fatigue on the final day but as long as anyone lived who had been a part of it, his memory of "The San'tary Fair" brought a sparkle to his eyes. Our friend W.S. Haven, the printer, published a little pamphlet entitled "The Pittsburgh Sanitary Fair," dated 1 June 1864 and authored by "An Old Citizen."

> Say! What is that building that stands on the green,
> Where the Stars and the Stripes proudly waving are seen?
> Is it meant for a market, or storage of grain,
> A political caucus, or theatre vain?
> 'Tis neither a market, nor grain elevator,
> A party convention, nor yet a theatre;
> Its purpose is one every heart must approve-
> Sweet Charity's Temple, the Bazaar of Love;
> Where, with zeal patriotic, the rich and the poor,
> All sects, and all parties, may mingle their store;
> Where all may contribute, by giving or buying,
> To succor the wounded, the sick or the dying-
> Our brave Volunteers, who in camp or on field,
> Like Napoleon's old vet'rans, may die! but ne'er yield.
> To recount all the articles here to be sold,
> Would a story as long as old Homer's unfold;
> But surely their taste most fastidious must be
> Who nothing to please it before them can see.
> Here are lots of substantials-bread, butter and cheese,
> And bright airy trifles the fancy to please;
> Here are carts, wagons, harrows, ploughs, mattocks and hoes,
> Shoes, notions, boots, stockings, and all sorts of clothes.
> For the ladies are ribbons, pins, cotton and lace,
> Bright mirrors where each may behold her sweet face,
> Embroideries, trimmings, thread, needles and tape,
> Chintzes, muslins, sacques, circulars, mantles and crape
> Handsome frocks for the children, fine shirts for the men.
> Don't you want a portfolio, or nice silver pen?
> Here are frying pans, gridirons, refrigerators,
> Churns, cheese presses, saddles and Japanese waiters.
> Of Iron there's pig, bloom, bar, boiler and rails,
> Anchors, anvils, spikes, log chains, and ten-penny nails.
> Should your favorite daughter desire a new toy,
> Here's a smartly dressed doll; or a horse for your boy.

Chessmen, dominoes, ninepins, to coaches and barrows,
Skipping ropes, kitchen furniture, tops, bows and arrow,
. . . . .
Here are clear crystal fountains, the thirst to assuage,
While neighbors and friends in sweet converse engage,
Old acquaintances meeting to part soon again;
Here are cups that oft cheer, ne'er inebriate the brain-
Coffee, chocolate, tea, with bright ladies to wait-
Sure never was royalty served in such state.
Ere we close, let us proper acknowledgments make
To all who have labored and toiled for our sake;
To the ladies, who gracefully here have displayed
Their genius and taste our exertions to aid;
To the children at school who have given their toys.
To comfort and cherish our Volunteer boys;
To the rich who have freely dispensed of their wealth;
To the givers in secret, who do good by stealth;
To the farmers, the merchants, mechanics and banks,
To each and to all we would tender our thanks.
And the blessings of those whom their labors have cheered
In whose memory their names will be ever endeared.
Oh think on the Soldier far distant who roams
And when to his country restored through your care,
Will grateful remember the San'tary Fair.[12] ★

HARPER'S WEEKLY.

A JOURNAL OF CIVILIZATION.

VOL. X.—No. 511.]

NEW YORK, SATURDAY, OCTOBER 13, 1866.

[SINGLE COPIES TEN CENTS.
$4.00 PER YEAR IN ADVANCE.

SOLDIERS' AND SAILORS' CONVENTION AT PITTSBURG.

THE Soldiers' and Sailors' Convention at Cleveland has met the same fate as the Philadelphia Convention of August 14. Neither of these Conventions were successful in their aims. They were, indeed, an expression of sentiments which responded to those of a large portion of our people. But, as the event proves, they did not touch the practical and immediate question before the people. They had their influence, but they did not create a new party. The Democratic party, condemned in every successive election since that of 1860, during the war insisted upon its claims to popular support, in a manner extremely offensive to all patriots; and now it has determined to reiterate these claims and calculates upon the prestige of Presidential support as a certain condition to its triumph. But the people have spoken in Maine and Vermont, and their verdict is clearly against trusting to the Democratic party the restoration of the country to peace. The case stands simply thus: the people are compelled to choose between a party which has carried them triumphantly through the most troublous and critical period of our history, and a party whose immediate antecedents excite their most hearty indignation.

It is at such a political turning-point that a Convention of soldiers and sailors has been held at Pittsburg, the assembling of which we illustrate on our first page.

The Convention met September 26. The evening previous there had been a torch-light procession. It was an occasion of popular excitement and enthusiasm scarcely paralleled in even the processions of our great metropolis. At an early hour on the morning of the 25th the City Hall of Pittsburg was

GEN. J. D. COX, PRESIDENT OF THE SOLDIERS' AND SAILORS' CONVENTION AT PITTSBURG.
[PHOTOGRAPHED BY ANTHONY.]

thronged with an enthusiastic audience, of whom a good proportion were ladies.

An eloquent speech was made by General MOODY.

At twelve o'clock General NEGLEY called the Convention to order, and General FRANCIS F. BARLOW, after the delivery of a prayer by Rev. GRANVILLE MOODY, read the call of the Convention.

In the afternoon General JACOB D. COX, of Ohio, whose portrait we give herewith, and whose military record has been one of great and deserved distinction, was chosen President of the Convention. He took the chair, which had been temporarily occupied by L. EDWIN DUDLEY, a private of the Thirteenth Massachusetts, and made a brief speech, in which he insisted that Congress had the sole right to determine upon the conditions of restoration.

General BUTLER, Chairman of the Committee on Resolutions, reported the following platform, which was unanimously adopted:

Resolved, That the action of the present Congress in passing the pending Constitutional Amendment is wise, prudent, and just. It clearly defines American citizenship, and guarantees all his rights to every citizen. It places on a just and equal basis the right of representation, making the vote of a man in one State equally potent with the vote of another man in any State. It righteously excludes from places of honor and trust the chief conspirators, guiltiest rebels, whose perjured crimes have drenched the land in fraternal blood. It puts into the very frame of our Government the inviolability of the National Debt, and the nullity forever of all obligations contracted in support of the rebellion.

Resolved, That it is unfortunate for the country that these propositions have not been received in the spirit of conciliation, clemency, and fraternal feeling in which they were offered, as they are the mildest terms ever granted to the subdued rebels.

Resolved, That the President, as an executive officer, has no right to a policy as against the Legislative Department of the Government, that his attempt to fasten his scheme of reconstruction upon the country was dangerous as it is unwise; his acts in sustaining it have retarded the restoration of peace and unity; they

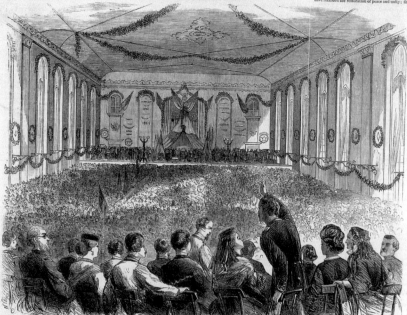

MEETING OF THE SOLDIERS' AND SAILORS' CONVENTION AT PITTSBURG, PENNSYLVANIA.—[SKETCHED BY C. S. REINHART.]

CHAPTER 8

THE PITTSBURGH SOLDIERS' AND SAILORS' CONVENTION, 25-26 SEPTEMBER 1866

BY CHARLES D. CASHDOLLAR

The end of the American Civil War signified the beginning of a heated, post-war political debate over the conditions by which the southern states would be readmitted to the Union. Arguing that secession was an unconstitutional act and that the South had never truly left the United States, President Abraham Lincoln supported a moderate reconstruction policy that provided for a relatively easy, non-punitive transition for the southern states. Andrew Johnson, Lincoln's successor and a southerner by birth, also backed a lenient stance on the Reconstruction issue. Radical Republicans in Congress, on the contrary, argued that the South was, in essence, a conquered province and should be treated more harshly than the Lincoln/Johnson plans dictated. In this essay, Charles Cashdollar provides a detailed overview of the Pittsburgh Soldiers' and Sailors' Convention of 1866, a lesser-known political event that reflected the growing schism between Radical Republicans and President Andrew Johnson and represented the first stage in the process by which Union veterans became a significant voting bloc in the post-war era. This essay first appeared in the October 1965 *Western Pennsylvania Historical Magazine*.

Left: A portion of a sketch by C.S. Reinhart of the Pittsburgh Soldiers' and Sailors' Convention as it appeared in the 13 October 1866 *Harper's Weekly*, which noted that the hall "was thronged with an enthusiastic audience, of whom a good portion were ladies." — HSWP Library & Archives

THE CITY OF PITTSBURGH PLAYED AN IMPORTANT ROLE IN THE STRUGGLE over reconstruction following the Civil War. During the late summer of 1866, President Andrew Johnson, in an attempt to present his policies personally to the people, toured the Northern states. During this "swing around the circle," Johnson repeatedly allowed himself to be drawn into impromptu exchanges with the extremist elements of his audience. When Johnson visited Pittsburgh on 13 September 1866, on his Northern tour, the mayor of the city refused to see him and an ill-mannered, jeering crowd refused to allow him to speak.[1] This visit to Pittsburgh was, as was the rest of Johnson's tour, extremely damaging to his cause. Even more injurious to the President' efforts, however, was the Soldiers' and Sailors' Convention held in Pittsburgh on 25 and 26 September 1866.

This convention was national in scope. Delegates arrived from as far away as California and Nevada.[2] To James G. Blaine, it was the most influential of the four political conventions held that year and it "... did more to popularize the Fourteenth Amendment as a political issue than any instrumentality of the year."[3] As such, it was extremely important in focusing the power struggle between President Johnson and the Radical Republicans in Congress.

The power struggle between Johnson and Congress began during the summer of 1865. Immediately upon his ascension to the Presidency, Johnson continued the reorganization of the Southern states which President Lincoln had begun. Congressional leaders watched his activity with great interest, some hoping for a more stringent policy toward the South than that of the late President Lincoln. By the time Congress met in December, however, it was evident that Johnson was following the lenient policies of his predecessor.

One small group of Congressmen, led by Thaddeus Stevens of Pennsylvania, was appalled by Johnson's actions. They plotted the establishment of a Congressional Committee on Reconstruction in an attempt to place control of the Southern question in the hands of the national legislature.[4] As the Thirty-Ninth Congressional session progressed, these men ruthlessly pushed to realize their aims.

At this stage Johnson still had sufficient support to achieve at least a compromise with the extremists.[5] It was not, however, in the President's character to compromise. On 23 February 1866, he vetoed the new Freedman's Bureau Bill. Then, on 27 March 1866, he vetoed the Civil Rights Bill passed by Congress. Each veto widened the schism developing between the Chief Executive and the Congress.

These Presidential vetoes, coupled with the superb political exploitation of events in the South by the Radicals, drove the moderates slowly, one-by-one, away from Johnson and into the extremist camp. By 9 April 1866, the Radicals had sufficient strength to pass the Civil Rights Bill over the President's veto. The necessary two-thirds majority now secured, the Radicals proceeded to pass the Fourteenth Amendment against the protests of Johnson. On 16 July they forced the Freedman's Bureau Bill over Johnson's veto. By mid-July even part of the President's Cabinet deserted him as three members resigned their positions and threw their support to the Radicals.[6]

When the Thirty-Ninth Congress adjourned on 28 July 1866, the split between the Republican leaders in Congress and President Johnson was nearly complete. Congress had become openly antagonistic to Johnson and his program of Southern restoration. The lines were drawn. In the fall elections both Johnson and the Congressional leaders would carry their programs to the people.

Lacking the benefit of an organized party machine, Johnson and his followers called a convention in the late summer to amass the necessary support to carry the fall elections. Specifically, James G. Blaine stated that they hoped to "...effect a complete consolidation of the Administration Republicans and the Democratic party."[7] The National Union Convention, as it was called, assembled in Philadelphia on 14 August 1866. Delegates were mainly well-known Democrats and a few conservative Republicans, such as Montgomery Blair and Henry Raymond. Clement

Vallandigham, the Civil War "copperhead," arrived to lend his support to the convention, but wisely yielding to the protests of the other delegates, he did not participate.[8]

The convention claimed to be the only group which reflected the interests of both the North and the South. Symbolizing this theme, Governor James L. Orr of South Carolina and General Darius N. Couch of Massachusetts marched into the convention hall arm-in-arm followed by their delegations.[9] The Resolutions Committee, under the chairmanship of Edgar Cowan of Pennsylvania, presented a platform supporting the common policies of the Administration and the Democratic party. It advocated the right of *all* States to be represented in Congress and denied the right of Congress to make laws for the South without its presence.[10]

Radical Republicans were not a little concerned at the image portrayed by the Johnson supporters at the Philadelphia convention. Immediately they organized a convention to counter the claim that this Johnson alliance was the only truly national party.[11] They decided to meet in Philadelphia on 3 September 1866. Delegations arrived from both the North and the South. The Northern delegates included such prominent men as Horace Greeley and John Jacob Astor from New York, Carl Schurz from Michigan, and Lyman Trumbull from Illinois. The Southern delegations were mainly composed of carpetbaggers. North Carolina, for example, had only two natives among its seven delegates.[12] Significantly, the two groups met separately, the Northerners under the chairmanship of Pennsylvania's Governor Andrew Curtin and the Southerners under former Attorney-General James Speed.

The chaplain set the tone for the proceeding in his opening prayer, asking for deliverance from the "... rule of bad men, especially from him [Johnson] who through satanic agency has been raised to authority over us."[13] The convention, centering its discussion around the Fourteenth Amendment, produced a series of vindictive charges against President Johnson. The Southerners asked for Northern protection from Johnson' traitorous governments and denounced the Administration's liberal use of its pardoning power. Speed, who a few short months before was a member of the Johnson Cabinet, urged Congress to continue its fight against the President because "... whenever you have a Congress that does not resolutely and firmly refuse, as the present Congress has done, to merely act as the recording secretary of the tyrant at the White House, American liberty is gone forever."[14] Successful in its attempt to counter the claims of Johnson's National Union Convention, this second Philadelphia convention greatly increased the strength of the anti-Johnson forces.[15]

Johnson' followers realized that their attempt to organize an effective force behind the President had failed. They then turned their attention to the former

Union soldiers in an attempt to draw a significant number of them away from the radicals.[16] These veterans were invited to meet in Cleveland, Ohio, on 17 September 1866. The convention which ensued was relatively weak and ineffective. It was chaired by General John Ellis Wool, the oldest major-general in the regular army, who, according to James Blaine, was under the impression that the convention was being held to prevent the abolitionists from declaring another war on the South. Composed mainly of delegates who were already members of the Democratic party, the convention drew very little support away from the Radical Republicans.[17]

As soon as it became apparent that the Johnson supporters were meeting in Cleveland, the veterans supporting the Radicals organized a convention so that their opinions might also be heard. The call went out for all honorably discharged Union soldiers and sailors who opposed Johnson and would "vote as they shot" to meet in Pittsburgh on 25 September 1866.[18]

On Sunday, 23 September 1866, Union veterans began to pour into the twin cities [Pittsburgh and Allegheny] at the confluence of the Allegheny and Monongahela Rivers. Nearly every state in the Union was represented as well as many of the territories. Delegates arrived from as far north as Maine and Vermont, from as far west as California and Nevada, and from as far south as Texas and Louisiana. Neighboring Ohio sent 500 delegates and a fine delegation arrived from Wisconsin with its famous eagle, "Honest Abe."[19] James Blaine estimated that 25,000 veterans were present.[20] In addition to the large number of former enlisted men, many distinguished officers were also present, including Generals Benjamin Butler, Robert Schenck, Franz Sigel and Nathaniel Banks.[21] Two other well-known officers sent their best regards to the delegates via telegraph: General John A. Logan who had planned to attend but was taken ill at the last moment, and General John C. Fremont whose invitation was mistakenly sent to St. Louis rather than New York and then not forwarded in time for his attendance.[22] Radial leaders proudly boasted that a "… body more pre-eminent has never been convened on this continent."[23]

Elaborate preparations under the efficient direction of General James S. Negley, head of the Residence Committee, had been made for the convention.[24] A huge temporary shelter, capable of seating 5,000 persons, was built on West Common south of Ohio Street. Its open sides permitted thousands gathered outside to hear the proceedings as well as those seated inside.[25]

The citizens of Pittsburgh left the attractions of the County Fair which was drawing to a close to render a hearty welcome to these "boys in blue." Nearly all the city's merchants decorated their storefronts and buildings with evergreens, flags, pictures, and mottoes in welcome to the veterans. The *Gazette*, Pittsburgh's Radical

Republican newspaper, caustically remarked that only two buildings on Fifth Avenue were not decorated — the United States Post Office and the office of the *Post*, Pittsburgh's Democratic newspaper.[26] The *Post* replied in its Thursday, 27 September edition that it was not the least sorry for not having decorated its office building. It had used up all its flags the preceding week when Andrew Johnson had been in Pittsburgh under the "… delusion that it was the duty as [sic] all well-bred citizens to pay some respect to the President of the United States, Mr. Johnson, the only one we believe now holding that office."[27]

One bit of merriment resulted from the decorations placed on the various office buildings. The *Gazette* had its offices on a second floor directly above the offices of the *Democrat*, a conservative German newspaper. The *Democrat*, which was supporting Hiester Clymer, the Democratic candidate for governor of Pennsylvania, hung a sign outside its office reading "Johnson and Clymer." The *Gazette* seized this opportunity to promote its cause at the expense of its rival downstairs and hung out a sign reading "Brave Men Detest." When the employees of the *Democrat* realized that the signs now read "Brave Men Detest Johnson and Clymer," they had the last laugh by replacing their sign "Johnson and Clymer" with the name of John W. Geary, the Republican candidate for governor.[28] The *Gazette*, finding itself outsmarted, agreed to end the little duel by removing its sign.[29]

City Hall, where the convention's opening business was transacted, was also decorated with evergreens, shields, mottoes, banners, and flags. The speaker's platform was enlarged by adding 16 feet to each side of it. Outside City Hall a huge triumphal arch had been built across Federal Street. At its top, some 30 feet above the pavement, was a large eagle.[30] The correspondent of the *New York Tribune* remarked that these decorations surpassed anything that he had seen at either of the two Philadelphia conventions.[31] The editors of the *Gazette* boasted proudly that this day was "… second only to the Fourth of July 1776. The Soldier's and Sailors' Convention is altogether unmatched by any similar demonstration on this continent."[32]

The city of Pittsburgh provided music for the festivities. A choir of 200 voices entertained the delegates at City Hall with selected patriotic and sacred songs. Even this music took an anti-Johnson air, however, as Professor J.W. Pope sang a satirical melody entitled "My Policy."[33]

The festive air permeated the entire city. So many people gathered at City Hall on the evening of 24 September, that an impromptu meeting was organized and speeches given for the entertainment of the crowd. As early as seven o'clock the next morning, citizens rushed to City Hall to see the decorations and to hear a poem entitled "The Veteran" read by its author, Colonel Edward Jay Allen of Pittsburgh.

The group was so large and unruly that there was considerable trouble getting the hall cleared for the beginning of the convention at noon.[34]

On Tuesday evening, 25 September, the festivities reached their climax with a magnificent torchlight parade. A great mass of soldiers, wagons, Chinese lanterns, banners, and horses passed through the streets of Pittsburgh to the music of bands and drum corps. Many of the marchers carried placards with such captions as "Congress is our Moses" as they moved through the city.[35]

According to statistics printed in the *Pittsburgh Gazette*, the parade included some 200 wagons, 2,500 horses, and some 15,000 veterans and private citizens.[36] Even allowing for undoubted Republican exaggeration, the event would appear successful. The pro-Johnson *New York Times* described the parade as "… immensely long and … interspersed with banners and mottoes, most various and appropriate. Strangers who have witnessed processions of this kind in other cities say they have never seen anything to compare with it in splendor."[37] Even the Democratic *Post* recorded that the procession took 55 minutes to pass a given point — hardly the "fizzle" which it called the demonstration.[38] Instead, this show of anti-Administration strength must be regarded as a successful expression of the enthusiasm evident that week in Pittsburgh.

The convention was called to order at noon on 25 September 1866, by General James S. Negley. Private L. Edwin Dudley was elected temporary chairman. Originally from Massachusetts, Dudley had been employed by the Treasury Department in Washington. When he applied for the three days vacation due him so that he might attend the convention in Pittsburgh, he was refused by the Administration officials. Dudley thereupon resigned his position and came to the convention where he was rewarded for his sacrifice by being made temporary chairman.[39] His resignation emphasized the importance which Union veterans placed on the convention and the Radical cause. This stubborn dedication to the Radical movement, which Dudley so well portrayed, was a major reason for the ultimate success of the convention.

In his acceptance speech, Dudley stated his firm belief that the convention would agree upon a denunciation of President Johnson and his policies that would "… sweep over the country in loud thunder tones, and … swell the majorities for the Union cause in all the Northern states."[40] After electing Governor Jacob Cox of Ohio permanent president of the convention, the delegates set out in vociferous agreement to denounce Johnson and his policies.

This attack on Johnson began with a delegate from Kansas who proposed three cheers for John Brown's body and promised that if "… Andrew Johnson will swing around the circle as far as Kansas, ... we will jayhawk him."[41] General John Gibbon in a speech before the convention mocked Johnson: "O! everyone who thirsteth come and worship me, and I will give him a post office."[42] One soldier who had lost part of each arm during the War testified that he had been refused a job by the President. This example of "my policy" was greeted with loud jeers.[43] The *Gazette* claimed that Johnson had as his motto: "We honor treason and detest loyalty."[44]

A letter from New Orleans was read to the delegates. It warned that the South had not been "sufficiently whipped" and that another war was imminent.[45] Inflamed by the letter and other reports from the South, the convention proceeded to advocate a harsh program for the restoration of the Southern States. General James Cochrane of New York, in an informal speech in his hotel, remarked that "there can be no lasting peace until the South is chained down, revolutionized, Yankeeized."[46] All regard for law and order seemed to be forgotten as the delegates planned their revenge on the South. One veteran commented: "To hell with the Constitution, we can make a new one."[47]

The angry frenzy of the denunciations came to a climax Wednesday afternoon, 26 September, when the report of the Resolutions Committee was presented by its chairman, General Benjamin Butler.[48] The resolutions presented supported the Congressional plan of reconstruction and asserted that the President had no right to an independent plan or policy. They urged support for the loyal Southerners and declared that the former Confederate states were the rightful prey of the doctrine of conqueror's rights. The resolutions were adopted unanimously without debate.[49] (Full text of these resolutions appears at the end.)

After presenting the resolutions, General Butler spoke for three-quarters of an hour with the angry sarcasm which typified the entire convention. Commenting on the position of the South, Butler said they had definitely been out of the Union and even:

> ... if they were not at that time out of the Union, certain it's that all the Union was out of them. (Laughter) I do not discuss the question what you call them. I deal with the question fully and firmly what they are. You may call them territories, conquered provinces — anything but our *governors*. I won't stand that. Is there any man here who will claim that by surrender, men got rights? Is there any man here who will claim that a man conquers by saying "I give up"?... The Congress of the United States ... have full right to make any necessary rules and regulations for the government of those camps of paroled prisoners of war!... In this great contest not one right of the government over these States and over their citizens was lost but every right of every traitor on the soil was forfeited and gone forever. Extend towards the South and the Southern men who,

as communities, have been misled, our cordial welcome back, when they will come back in the spirit of justice, of regret, of kindness, and of loyalty with which we offer to receive them.... And until that time comes, be it sooner of later, till every man can walk in peace carrying, if he pleases, the flag of the United States with devotion to the Union on his lips and not be molested in any revolted State, for one I do not want to see that State in the Union making laws for me.[50]

Continuing his speech, Butler advocated the hanging of Robert E. Lee and Jefferson Davis. At the mention of Lee's name cries of "Hang him!" "Shoot him!" "No! not a soldier's death!" rang through the hall.[51] Butler said that Davis had "... played for an empire — he staked his life upon the result and let him pay the forfeit (great applause) as an example for all time that no man shall plot treason in the halls of the Congress of the United States."[52]

Butler then turned his attention to another "traitor" — Andrew Johnson. He blamed Johnson for encouraging and fostering Southern insolence and urged his fellow soldiers to make it clear to the South that "... the President don't [sic] rule this country without the aid of Congress."[53]

Butler commented at length on the insolence of the South. He called the attention of the delegates to the desecration of Union graves in the South and shouted furiously that "we shall not have those States brought back into the Union until our dead comrades can sleep in peace and honor within their graves. And if any man wants reconstruction before that happens, I am not willing for one."[54]

After Butler's fiery speech, the convention observed a moment of silence for Lincoln whose "... life was taken by the men who now claim for equal rights with us in the administration of the Government," gave three cheers for Grant, Sherman, Sheridan, and Farragut, and the adjourned *sine die*.[55]

Dudley's wish for a vicious denunciation of the President was fulfilled. The convention had dealt severely with Johnson. The details of this attack were spread throughout the nation by the press. Reporters attended the convention from New York, Boston, Cincinnati, Indianapolis, Chicago, St. Louis, Philadelphia, Milwaukee and other cities.[56] The *New York Tribune* stated that the convention had reason to be praised as the greatest ever held,[57] and the *New York Times*, despite its pro-Johnson leanings, carried a three and one-half column description of the convention on 26 September and on the following day reprinted the speech of General Butler and the report of the Committee on Resolutions.[58]

The delegates themselves, mirroring the enthusiasm of Private Dudley, did much to spread the policies of the convention. After their return home, each of the delegates received a copy of the proceedings by mail.[59] The elaborate displays at Pittsburgh had greatly impressed the delegates and had helped to consolidate "... almost *en masse* the soldiers of the country in support of the Republican party as represented by Congress."[60]

Before the convention adjourned, General Negley spoke to the delegates, stating that:

> You will take care of the American Union. I can further say that you have still another round in your cartridge boxes, another arrow in your bosom, to shoot the Gester [sic] who dares to raise his cap on the pole of despotism above the will of the American people for them to bow to.[61]

The "boys in blue," in truth, did have another cartridge in their boxes — it was a verbal one, a psychological one — but nevertheless a deadly one. Many of the veterans who had been to Pittsburgh returned home and delivered speeches concerning their wonderful experiences at the convention and the dreadful policies of President Johnson that they had discussed.[62] The soldiers made it quite clear to their fellow citizens that they had not fought "... for a Union in which it is possible for confessed rebels to wear the highest honors and to dominate in the highest councils."[63] They also made it quite clear that this is what they thought would be the result of Johnson's program.

In 1866 the Union soldiers and sailors were, as are all returning heroes, highly respected men in their communities.

> Their enthusiasm was greater, their feeling more intense, their activity more marked than could be found among the civilians of the country who were supporting the same principles.... Their convention, their expressions, their determination were felt throughout the entire Union as an aggressive, irresistible force.... Not even the Members of Congress, who repaired to their districts with the Fourteenth Amendment as the leading question, could recommend it to the mass of voters with the strength and with the good results which attended the soldier orators who were inspired to enter the field.[64]

It was the Pittsburgh Convention which rallied and consolidated the Union soldiers and sailors into an effective political force. More than any other single event, it signaled the entrance of the old soldier influence into post-Civil War politics, an influence that was to dominate the American scene for the remainder of the century.[65]

The American people willingly followed the advice of these veterans. In the Congressional election of 1866, the Radical Republicans in Congress secured a solid victory. It is impossible to overestimate the significance of this election. President Johnson and his policy were defeated; the South would undergo the scourge of Radical Reconstruction.

REPORT OF THE COMMITTEE ON RESOLUTIONS

Resolved, That the action of the present Congress in proposing the pending Constitutional amendments is wise, patriotic and just.

It clearly defines American citizenship and guarantees all the rights of every citizen.

It places on a just and equal basis the right of representation, making the vote of a man in one State equally potent with the vote of another man in any other State.

It righteously excludes from places of honor and trust the chief conspirators and guiltiest rebels whose perjured crimes have drenched the land in fraternal blood.

It puts into the very frame of our Government the inviolability of the national debt, and the nullity forever of all obligations contracted in support of the rebellion.

Resolved, That it is unfortunate for the country that those propositions have not been received in the spirit of conciliation, clemency and fraternal feeling in which they were offered as they are the mildest terms ever offered to subdued rebels.

Resolved, That the President, as an Executive officer, has no right to a policy as against the Legislative Department of the Government. That his attempt to fasten his scheme of reconstruction upon the country is a usurpation as dangerous as it is unwise. His acts in sustaining it have retarded the restoration of peace and unity. They have converted conquered rebels into impudent claimants for rights which they have forfeited and places which they have desecrated. If consummated it would render the sacrifice of the nation useless; the loss of lives of our buried comrades vain; and the war in which we have so gloriously triumphed what his present friends at Chicago in 1864 have declared it to be — a failure.

Resolved, That the rights of the conquerors to legislate for the conquered has been recognized by the public law of all civilized nations. By the operation of that law for the conservation of the highest good of the whole country, Congress has the undoubted right to establish measures for the conduct of the revolted states and to do all acts of legislation that are necessary for the complete restoration of the Union.

Resolved, That when the President claims that by the aid of the army and navy he might have made himself dictator, he insulted every soldier and sailor of the Republic. He ought distinctly to understand that the tried patriots of this nation can never be used to overthrow civil liberty in popular governments.

Resolved, That the neutrality laws should be amended as to give the fullest liberty to the citizens consistent with the national faith: That the great Union Republican party is pledged to maintain liberty and equality of rights everywhere, and therefore we tender to all peoples struggling for freedom, our sympathy and cordial cooperation.

Resolved, That the Union men of the South, without distinction of race and color, are entitled to the gratitude of every loyal soldier and sailor who served his country in suppressing the rebellion; and that in their present dark hour of trial, when they are being murdered and persecuted by thousands, solely because they are now and have been true to the Government, we will not prove recreant to our obligations, but will stand by and protect with our lives, if necessary, those brave men who remained true to us when all around were false and faithless.

Resolved, That the public domain as the common property of the nation, ought to be sacredly held donated to the benefit of the nation's defenders; that Congress ought to legislate in regard to bounties and pensions, with the most exact and impartial justice to all soldiers and sailors.

Resolved, That in the organization of the army and navy, the volunteer officers and soldiers demand that the faithful service in the field ought to be held equivalent to an education at West Point.

Resolved, That any officer, soldier or sailor, who left his flag to serve with our enemies, ought never to have place in the army or navy of the Union.

Source: *Pittsburgh Gazette*
27 September 1866 ★

NOTES

CHAPTER 1
WESTERN PENNSYLVANIA AND THE ELECTION OF 1860

BY JOSEPH P. WOLSTONCRAFT

1   Official Returns, *Pittsburgh Gazette*, 22 October 1860.
2   Ibid., 23 November 1860. [The most widely used and reliable voting statistics for the 1860 election are found in Horace Greeley's *Tribune Almanac of 1861*. According to this source, Lincoln received a 59,618 majority over all opposition. Curtin, meanwhile, received 32,164].
3   *Pittsburgh Evening Chronicle*, 10 October 1860.
4   John G. Nicolay and John Hay, *Abraham Lincoln, Complete Works* (New York: Century Compus, 1894), 1:584.
5   *Gazette*, 28 January; 11 February; 11 May; 18 September 1860; *Chronicle*, 8 October 1860; *Pittsburgh Post*, 29 February 1860.
6   *Gazette*, 21 August 1860.
7   *Chronicle*, 8 October 1860.
8   Ibid., 31 July 1860.
9   Ibid., 22 November 1859.
10   *Gazette*, 26 January 1860.
11   Ibid., 9 February 1860.
12   Letter to W.E. Frazer, Nicolay and Hay, *Abraham Lincoln, Complete Works*, 1:575.
13   *Gazette*, 24 and 25 February 1860.
14   Ibid., 24 February 1860.
15   Ibid., 1 March 1860.
16   J.F. Rhodes, *History of the United States* (New York: The Macmillan Company, 1930), 2:459.
17   *Gazette*, 19 May 1860.
18   Ibid., 21 May 1860.
19   Ibid., 19 May 1860.
20   Ibid., 11 February 1860.
21   Ibid., 31 May 1860.
22   Ibid., 19 May 1860.
23   Ibid.
24   *The Washington Reporter*, 24 May 1860.
25   *Gazette*, 28 May 1860.
26   Ibid., 5 June 1860 and 28 May 1860.
27   The *Washington Review*, a Democratic paper, favored this withdrawal. It says, on 10 May 1860, "The temporary secession of the fire eating disunion school of politicians ... promises nothing but good results.... We believe we are stronger to-day in the South without the aid of Yancy and Co."
28   *Post*, 15 June 1860.
29   Ibid., 25 June 1860.
30   Ibid., 6 July 1860.
31   *Gazette*, 17 October 1860.
32   J.G. Blaine, *Twenty Years of Congress* (Norwich, Conn.: Henry Bill Pub. Co., 1884), 2:206.
33   Ibid., 2:205f.
34   Platform of Allegheny County Republican Convention, *Post*, 5 January 1860.
35   *Gazette*, 23 February 1860.
36   *Reporter*, 7 March 1860; *Gazette*, 9 October 1860.
37   *Post*, 17 April 1860; 19 and 25 September 1860.

38 J.G. Blaine, *Twenty Years of Congress*, 1:205.
39 Republican: *Gazette*, 24 February 1860; *Post*, 5 January 1860. Democratic: *Post*, 7 June 1860 and 25 September 1860. For a detailed discussion of the tariff question, see I.F. Boughter, "Western Pennsylvania and the Morill Tariff," *Western Pennsylvania Historical Magazine*, 6 (April 1923): 106 – 33.
40 *Reporter*, 8 January 1860; Address to the People of Pennsylvania by the Republican State Convention, *Gazette*, 25 February 1860; Speech by Mr. Armor in Pittsburgh, *Gazette*, 22 February 1860 and 28 September 1860.
41 *Gazette*, 6 November 1860.
42 Ibid., 25 February 1860.
43 *Gazette*, 6 October 1860.
44 Ibid., 22 February 1860.
45 Blaine, *Twenty Years of Congress*, 1:205.
46 Ibid., 1:206
47 Quoted by *Gazette*, 9 October 1860.
48 Ibid., 11 June 1860.
49 *Gazette*, 28 September 1860.
50 Ibid., 18 June 1860.
51 Ibid., 9 October 1860, quoting the *Philadelphia North American*.
52 *Post*, 5 March 1860; see also *Gazette*, 3 March 1860.
53 *Post*, 25 September 1860.
54 Ibid., 30 April 1860.
55 Ibid., 31 July 1860; 15 September 1860.
56 Ibid., 31 May 1860; 7 and 14 June 1860.
57 Ibid., 23 October 1860.
58 Ibid., 2 November 1860.
59 *Gazette*, 22 February 1860.
60 Ibid., 30 June 1860.
61 *Post*, 26 January 1860.
62 Ibid., 10 January 1860.
63 *Gazette*, 3 July 1860.
64 Ibid., 11 July 1860, quoting the *Greensburg Argus*.
65 Ibid., 6 July 1860.
66 Ibid., 11 July 1860, quoting the *Greensburg Argus*.
67 Ibid., 16 July, 1860.
68 Ibid., 13 July 1860.
69 Ibid., 28 July 1860.
70 Ibid., 11 August 1860.
71 Ibid.
72 Ibid., 3 September 1860.
73 *Chronicle*, 16 August 1860.
74 *Post*, 17 August 1860.
75 *Gazette*, 17 and 20 August 1860; *Post*, 17 August 1860.
76 *Post*, 20 October 1860.
77 Official returns, *Gazette*, 22 October 1860. The result in the other counties of Western Pennsylvania was as follows:

County	Curtin	Foster
Fayette	3,382	3,556
Greene	1,529	2,669
Somerset	2,977	1,372
Indiana	3,672	1,886
Armstrong	3,474	2,698
Lawrence	2,645	959
Mercer	3,624	2,794

Venango	2,581	2,142
Clarion	1,795	2,297
Crawford	5,277	3,178
Erie	5,613	2,469
Warren	2,112	1,172

78 Official returns, *Gazette*, 23 November 1860. The result in the other counties was as follows:

County	Lincoln	Fusion	Douglas	Bell
Fayette	3,454	3,308	24	147
Greene	1,614	2,665	26	17
Somerset	3,218	1,175	—	1
Indiana	3,910	1,347	—	22
Armstrong	3,355	2,108	—	50
Lawrence	2,937	788	16	31
Mercer	3,855	2,546	2	49
Venango	2,680	1,932	6	6
Clarion	1,829	2,078	—	12
Crawford	5,779	2,961	62	—
Erie	6,160	2,531	17	90
Warren	2,284	1,087	4	—

CHAPTER 3

CAMP WILKINS, MILITARY POST, 1861

BY JOSEPH A. BORKOWSKI

1   *Pittsburgh Post*, 16 April 1861.

2   *Pittsburgh Gazette*, 16 April 1861.

3   *Pittsburgh Post*, 18 April 1861.

4   One of Pittsburgh's most distinguished civic and political leaders of the day. At the time of the outbreak of the Civil War, Wilkins was the Chairman of the Committee of One Hundred, which directly assumed provisioning and quartering all volunteers. Wilkins was born in Carlisle on 20 December 1779, was President of the Common Council of Pittsburgh, served in the State Legislature, was Judge of the Fifth Judicial District of Pennsylvania, appointed Minister to Russia, appointed Secretary of War from 15 February 1844 to 4 November 1845, and in 1855 elected to the United States Senate. He was the first President of the Bank of Pittsburgh. One contemporary news writer described him thus at the time of crisis: "With his silvery locks, his animated eyes, his clarion voice, his patriotic fire which eighty winters failed to lay chill, he exhorted his fellow citizens to lay aside all former differences and rally around the President." *Pittsburgh Gazette*, 16 April 1861.

5   *Pittsburgh Catholic*, 20 April 1861.

6   *Pittsburgh Post*, 18 April 1861.

7   The fair grounds proper were owned by the Harmar Denny Estate.

8   *Pittsburgh Gazette*, 29 April 1861.

9   Ibid., 16 April 1861.

10   *Pittsburgh Post*, 29 April 1861.

11   Ibid. Also printed in the *Pittsburgh Gazette*, 29 April 1861.

12   Ibid.

13   They were the Garibaldi Guards commanded by Captain Francis Hardtmeyer; Duncan Guards commanded by Captain John W. Duncan; Chartiers Valley Guards commanded by Captain Charles Barnes; Pittsburgh Rifles commanded by Captain Lewis W. Smith; Anderson Guards commanded by Captain George S. Hays; and the Iron City Guards commanded by Captain Charles M. Gormly. *Pittsburgh Gazette*, 2 May 1861.

14   Johnston was governor from 26 July 1848 to 20 January 1852.

15   Banker, industrialist, philanthropist and civic leader, Howe served in Congress from 1851 – 1853, was President of the Exchange Bank in 1852, and President of the Chamber of Commerce. He was very active during the Civil War period, named chairman of centralizing the recruitment of volunteers and later named as acting Adjutant General. Camp Howe, in the Oakland District, was named after him. His leadership and activities on behalf of enlisting recruits proved very effective, especially in 1862 when ardor to enlist was at its lowest. In private life he was secretary and treasurer of the North Cliff Mining Company and C.G. Hussey and Company, and of James Childs Company. *History of Allegheny County* (Chicago: A. Warner & Co., 1889), 239.

16   *Pittsburgh Post*, 2 May 1861.

17   *Pittsburgh Gazette*, 2 May 1861.

18   *Pittsburgh Post*, 3 May 1861.

19   *Pittsburgh Gazette*, 3 May 1861. Weaver was Mayor of Pittsburgh from 1857 – 1859.

20   *Pittsburgh Post*, 29 April 1861.

21   Ibid.

22   In the rear was the present lower part of Herron Hill below Brereton Avenue originating just above the Twenty-eighth Street Bridge and generally referred to as the Polish Hill; also in the same immediate area the Western Pennsylvania Hospital was located where the Citizens' Committee on Public Safety procured "an apartment for use and occupancy of sick soldiers at Camp Wilkins." *Pittsburgh Gazette*, 6 June 1861.

23   The Governors present were Andrew Curtin of Pennsylvania, William Denison of Ohio, Alexander Randall of Wisconsin, Austin Blair of Michigan, and Oliver Morton of Indiana. They met in Cleveland on 3 May. The purpose of the meeting was to reach an agreement for common defense against Confederate invasion. *Pittsburgh Catholic*, 11 May 1861.

24   *Pittsburgh Post*, 9 May 1861.

25   Ibid.

26   *Pittsburgh Gazette*, 20 May 1861.

27   Ibid., 14 May 1861.

28   Captain A.M. Judson, *History of the Eighty Third* (Erie: B.F.H. Lynn, no date), 22.

29   Ibid.

30   Ibid.

31   *Pittsburgh Gazette*, 21 May 1861.

32   Ibid., 22 May 1861 and *Pittsburgh Post*, 3 May 1861.

33   *Pittsburgh Gazette*, 22 May 1861.

34   Ibid., 27 May 1861.

35   Ibid., 18 June 1861.

36   Ibid., 13 June 1861.

37   See footnote 15.

38   *Pittsburgh Gazette*, 8 August 1861.

39   Ibid., 2 September 1861.

40   *Evening Chronicle*, 27 July, 5 August and 27 August 1861. It is almost impossible to trace the first names of some of the "officers" mentioned. Apparently they were organizers who were never commissioned.

41   *Pittsburgh Post*, 30 and 31 August 1861.

42   Alexander Schimmelfennig was born in Germany in 1824. He fought in the Hungarian Wars for independence under Lajos Kossuth and upon capitulation came to the United States. Commissioned Colonel 23 July 1861, he briefly led the Third Division of the Eleventh Corps in the Battle of Gettysburg. His forces were the first to enter Charleston on 18 February 1865 and also to take possession of Forts Sumter and Moultrie. He died at Minersville, Pennsylvania, 7 September 1865. He was mustered out with a rank of Brigadier General of volunteers and rates as one of the better field generals of the Army of the Potomac. Samuel P. Bates, *Martial Deeds of Pennsylvania* (Philadelphia: T.H. Davis and Co., 1876), 643.

43   *Pittsburgh Post*, 9 October 1861.

44   Ibid., 11 October 1861.

45 James S. Negley of Pittsburgh was born 26 December 1826. Enlisted as a private in the War with Mexico and, upon termination, returned to engage in horticulture. As a civilian he rendered important services in organizing and training local military companies in Allegheny County and at the time the Civil War broke out he already was in command of a brigade. He was frequently consulted by Governor A. Curtin on military affairs. For valor displayed at Cedar Forest, Negley was made Major General of the volunteers. In 1869, he was elected to Congress and twice re-elected. Bates, *Martial Deeds of Pennsylvania*, 949.

46 Frederick Shearer Stumbaugh, born in Franklin County, Pennsylvania, 14 April 1817. His regiment took part in battles under Buell in Kentucky and in support of Grant at Shiloh. Nominated by President Lincoln as Brigadier General, he resigned his commission following a lingering illness in December 1862. Later served as a member of the Pennsylvania Legislature. Bates, *Martial Deeds of Pennsylvania*, 881.

47 William Sirwell was born in Pittsburgh, 10 August 1820. He entered military service in 1839 and was in command of Pittsburgh Blues, Washington Blues, Brady Alpines, and Kittanning Yeagers. Brigade-Inspector of Armstrong County. Married to Miss Elizabeth McCandless on 6 November 1840. For distinguished military services during the Civil War, Sirwell was made Provost Marshal and later placed in command of Second Brigade, Fifteenth Division of the Fourteenth Corps. He was mustered out 4 November 1864. Bates, *Martial Deeds of Pennsylvania*, 931.

48 *Presbyterian Banner*, 26 October 1861.

49 *Pittsburgh Catholic*, 24 August 1861; *Pittsburgh Post*, 1 February 1862 and 3 February 1862. Camp Wright was sold at public auction on 3 February 1862.

50 There were officially five State Military Camps organized by the Commonwealth of Pennsylvania as of 1861: Camp Curtin near Harrisburg; Camp Washington at Easton; Camp Wayne at West Chester; Camp Wilkins at Pittsburgh; Camp Wright at Hulton. [Other Pittsburgh-area camps in existence between 1861 and 1864 included Camp Scott, Camp Fremont, Camp Howe, Camp Montgomery, Camp Copeland (later renamed Camp Reynolds), Camp Swearinger, and Camp Brooks].

51 *Pittsburgh Evening Chronicle*, 10 December 1861 and 18 December 1861.

52 *Pittsburgh Post*, 3 December 1861.

CHAPTER 4
GENERAL JAMES SCOTT NEGLEY

BY ALFRED P. JAMES

1 Genealogical information in John W. Jordan, *Encyclopedia of Pennsylvania Biography* (New York: Lewis Historical Publishing Company, 1915), 5:1635 f; and Georgina C. Negley, comp., *East Liberty Presbyterian Church: With Historical Setting and a Narrative of the Centennial Celebration, April 12 – 20, 1919* (Pittsburgh: Murdoch, Kerr & Co. Press, 1919). The information in the former reference is repeated verbatim in *History of Pittsburgh and Environs* (New York: American Historical Society, Inc., 1922), 4:57 f. Miss Georgina C. Negley is my authority for the acreage, sometimes placed at only a thousand acres.

2 *Year Book of the Pennsylvania Society of New York* (New York: Pennsylvania Society of New York, 1902), 75. Though they are probably not independent of each other, there is unanimous agreement on this item in the half dozen or more biographical sketches found in various biographical encyclopedias, albums and dictionaries.

3 Information furnished by Miss Georgina C. Negley and Mr. James R. Mellon.

4 Obituary statement in *Pittsburgh Press*, 8 October 1930, 5. It was a misfortune that an interview was not obtained with Mrs. Shillito before her death.

5 This information is found in several biographical sketches of General Negley, some of them published during his lifetime, and presumably is correct. It is interesting that the Alumni Secretary does not have a record of him.

6 *The Year Book of the Pennsylvania Society of New York*, 75, says he joined the Duquesne Greys at the age of 17. Other biographical sketches put the date two years later.

7   Ibid.
8   *Pennsylvania Archives*, Sixth Series, Volume 10, Harrisburg, 1907, 391. The *Pittsburgh Morning Post*, 18 December 1846, lists "J.S. Negley" as a private in the Duquesne Greys.
9   *Year Book of the Pennsylvania Society of New York*, 75.
10   *Pennsylvania Archives*, sixth series, volume 10, Harrisburg, 1907, 391. The reference says "4th Sergt."
11   Ibid.
12   Jordan, *Encyclopedia of Pennsylvania Biography*, 5:1639. In Woodward & Rowlands' *Pittsburgh Directory for 1852*, printed by W.S. Hanen, Book and Fancy Job Printer, Pittsburgh, there is the item, "Negley James, shovel manuf. at 152 Third St." Presumably this is a reference to James Scott Negley.
13   Jordan, *Encyclopedia of Pennsylvania Biography*, 5:1639. Dr. William J. Holland is authority for the fact that Negley maintained throughout life a great interest in flowers. Mr. P.W. Siebert, in comments made on hearing this paper read, stated that as a boy he used to get flowers at Mr. Negley's gardens.
14   Copies of the directories for these years are in the Central Carnegie Library of Pittsburgh.
15   Jordan, *Encyclopedia of Pennsylvania Biography*, 5:1639. *Pittsburgh Post*, 15 August 1859, mentions "Brigadier General Negley" as in charge of arrangements for a militia encampment. This paper two days later gives his General Orders No. 4, and praises his management and ability in highest terms. This praise is repeated 18 August 1859.
16   Ibid. According to *The Pittsburgh Post*, 14 February and 16 February 1861, Brigadier General Negley commanded "the military and civic procession" on President-elect Abraham Lincoln's famous arrival in Pittsburgh on 14 February 1861 and on his departure for Cleveland the following morning.
17   *Pittsburgh Dispatch*, 15 April 1861, 3; *Pittsburgh Post*, 15 April 1861, 1.
18   Ibid.
19   *Pittsburgh Dispatch*, 16 April 1861, 3.
20   Information based on local newspapers, 16 April 1861 and 24 April 1861.
21   *Pittsburgh Dispatch*, 18 April 1861; *Pittsburgh Gazette*, 23 April 1861, 3.
22   *Pittsburgh Gazette*, 25 April 1861; *Pittsburgh Post*, 25 April 1861.
23   Sarah H. Killikelly. *The History of Pittsburgh: Its Rise and Progress* (Pittsburgh: B.C. Gordon Montgomery Co., 1906), 429.
24   Samuel P. Bates, *History of Pennsylvania Volunteers, 1861 – 5* (Harrisburg: B. Singerly, 1869), 1:135.
25   *War of the Rebellion: A Compilation of the Official Records of the Union and Confederate Armies* (Washington, D.C.: Government Printing Office, 1880 – 1901), series 2, 635. Where, as in this case, the series is not given, it must be understood that the reference is to series 1. This publication will hereinafter be cited as *Rebellion Records*.
26   Ibid., 679, June 1861.
27   Ibid., 699.
28   Ibid., 709.
29   Ibid., 728, Negley to Porter, 28 June 1861.
30   Bates, *History of the Pennsylvania Volunteers*, 1:135.
31   *Rebellion Records*, series 2, 160.
32   Ibid., 164.
33   Ibid., series 3, volume 1, 358, Curtin to Cameron, 27 July 1861.
34   Ibid., 407, 13 August 1861, instructions from Washington, D.C., mentioning "such companies of volunteer infantry as may be presented to you by Brigadier-General Negley."
35   Ibid., 464.
36   Ibid., series 1, volume 4, 308.
37   Ibid., series 1, volume 5, 621, Thomas A. Scott to Negley, 16 October 1861; volume 4, 309, Scott to Negley, 17 October 1861.
38   Ibid., series 3, volume 1, 578, Curtin to Scott. On this review consult *The Pittsburgh Gazette*, 18 October 1861.
39   Ibid., series 1, volume 3, 548, L. Thomas to Cameron, 21 October 1861.
40   Ibid., series 3, volume 1, 578, Curtin to Scott, 17 October 1861; series 1, volume 2, Sherman to L. Thomas, 22 October 1861.

[41] Ibid., series 1, volume 4, 318, Sherman's Special Orders No. 67, 22 October 1861; series 1, volume 2, 332, Sherman to L. Thomas, 4 November 1861.

[42] Ibid., volume 2, 333.

[43] Ibid., volume 7, Special Orders, No. 16, 30 November 1861.

[44] Ibid., volume 7, 938. Buell to McCook, 13 February 1862.

[45] Ibid., volume 10, part 2, 71, Buell to Mitchel, 27 March 1862.

[46] Ibid., 86, Buell to Negley, 1 April 1862.

[47] Ibid., 161, Matthews to Campbell, 4 May 1862.

[48] Ibid., part 1, 894, Negley's report, 14 May 1862; 892, Mitchel's report, 15 May, 1862.

[49] Ibid., 892, Mitchel's report, 15 May 1862.

[50] Ibid., part 2, 257, Mitchel to Buell, 4 June 1862.

[51] Ibid., part 1, 920, Negley's reports.

[52] Ibid., 53, 54, 57, 62; part 2, 282, Buell to Halleck, 9 June 1862, 283, 288, 633, 634.

[53] Ibid., volume 16, part 2, 40, Greene to Fry, 20 June 1862.

[54] Ibid., 300, Negley to Fry, 9 August 1862.

[55] Ibid, part 1, 842 – 43, 859, reports of General Negley, 11 August 1862 and 14 August 1862.

[56] Ibid., part 2, 340 – 41, Fry to Negley, 15 August 1862.

[57] Ibid., 355, Buell to Negley, 18 August 1862; 378, Buell to Negley, 20 August 1862; 397, Fry to Negley, 23 August 1862. See similar orders, 398, 430, 437.

[58] Ibid., 511, Fry to Thomas.

[59] Ibid., 989.

[60] Ibid., 583, J.F. Boyle to Abraham Lincoln, 7 October 1862.

[61] Ibid., part 1, 1020 – 21, Negley's report, 9 October 1862.

[62] Ibid., part 2, 619, Negley to Fry, 15 October 1862.

[63] Ibid., 611, Buell to Halleck, 13 October 1862; 636 – 7, Buell to Halleck, 22 October 1862.

[64] Ibid., volume 20, part 1, 3 – 4, Negley's reports.

[65] Ibid., volume 16, part 1, 253, Testimony of Major Sedell, 25 December 1862.

[66] Ibid., volume 20, part 1, 406, f. Negley's report.

[67] Ibid.

[68] Ibid., 408.

[69] Ibid., volume 23, part 2, 83.

[70] Ibid., 196.

[71] Ibid., part 1, 442 – 44, report of 8 July 1863.

[72] Ibid., part 2, 394 – 95.

[73] Ibid., 407, 9 June 1863.

[74] Ibid., volume 30, part 3, 563, 12 September 1863.

[75] Ibid., part 1, 1016 and 1043, Court of Inquiry proceedings and finding. Negley's critics were Generals John M. Brennan and Thomas J. Wood.

[76] Ibid., 202.

[77] Ibid, 206 – 7.

[78] Ibid., 220.

[79] Bates, *History of the Pennsylvania Volunteers*, 2:1033.

[80] *Rebellion Records*, volume 30, part 1, 333, Rosecrans to L. Thomas, 14 October 1863.

[81] Ibid.

[82] Ibid., 362, Negley to Stanton, 29 October 1863.

[83] Ibid., volume 31, part 1, 60.

[84] Ibid., 63 – 64.

[85] Ibid.

[86] Ibid, volume 52, part 1, 506.

[87] Ibid., volume 30, part 1, 362.

[88] Ibid., 1004 – 44, record of the Negley Court of Inquiry, 29 January 1864. The verdict is found on the last two pages.

[89] Ibid., volume 52, part 1, 538.

90 I have been informed by Dr. William J. Holland of Pittsburgh who knew him well, that General Negley ever afterward cherished the sense of grievance at the injustice which he felt had been done him.

91 This assertion is based not only on the records of this case but on familiarity with many other cases.

92 On this matter, see Isaac R. Pennypacker, "Civil War Historians and History," *Pennsylvania Magazine of History and Biography*, 51 (1927), 330 – 350, esp, 334 – 335.

93 In Congress, 10 March 1870, Congressman Negley made a bitter sarcastic speech on West Pointers. See *Congressional Globe*, 41st Cong., 2nd Sess., 1850 f. The prompt rejoiner of Congressman Slocum must have indicated the futility of this procedure.

94 *Pittsburgh Directory for 1864 – 65*, 239.

95 Consult the Pittsburgh directories. Miss Georgina Negley says the Ellsworth Avenue site is now occupied by the Georgian Court Apartments.

96 *Pittsburgh Directory for 1869 – 70, 332; Pittsburgh Directory for 1886*, 704. Miss Georgina Negley is certain General Negley never lived on Fifth Avenue, near Highland.

97 *Congressional Globe*, Forty-first Cong., 1st Sess., 697 and 714.

98 Ibid., 505, 5 April 1869.

99 Ibid., 2nd Sess., 1,166; 1,232; 1,387 f.; 1,623; 1,855; 2,083; 2,330; 2,416; 3,582.

100 Ibid., 2,043.

101 Ibid., 2,722.

102 See long speech in the Appendix of this session, 334 – 40.

103 *Congressional Globe*, 41st Cong., 2nd Sess., 3,727.

104 Ibid., 1,163 – 64.

105 Ibid., 42nd Cong., 1st Sess., 188, 20 March 1871.

106 Ibid.

107 Ibid., Index.

108 Ibid., 2nd Sess., 393.

109 Ibid., 836; 976; 1962.

110 Ibid., 1,310.

111 Ibid., 1,400.

112 Ibid., 1,961.

113 Ibid., 2,050 f., 28 March 1872.

114 Ibid., 2,205, 5 April 1872.

115 Ibid., 3,513.

116 Ibid., 4,452.

117 Ibid., 3rd Sess., 221.

118 Ibid., 1,336. The speech is in the Appendix, 52 f.

119 Ibid., 43rd Cong, 1st Sess., 75.

120 Ibid., 62.

121 Ibid., 1,016, 31 January 1874.

122 Ibid., 1,255, 5 February 1874.

123 Ibid., 1,173; 1,825, 26 February 1874; 2,436, 24 March 1874; 1,825, 26 February 1874; 2,436, 24 March 1874; 3,564, 4 May 1874.

124 Ibid., 60, 109, 113 – 14.

125 Ibid., 2,195; 2,279 – 80; 2,455 – 57; 2,690 – 92.

126 Ibid., 91.

127 Ibid., 2,627.

128 Ibid., 3,851. As bearing on his legal knowledge, his daughter writes in 1930, "The City of New York employed him as an expert witness to fight railroad encroachments. He used to get large fees for his legal testimony, being considered an authority on such matters."

129 Ibid., 3,862.

130 Ibid., 5,403, 22 June 1874.

131 *Congressional Record*, 43rd Cong., 2nd Sess., 70, 14 December 1875.

132 Ibid., 358, 8 January 1875.

133 Ibid., 701, 25 January 1875.

134 Ibid., 1,033, 6 February 1875.

135 Ibid., 567, 18 January 1875; 905, 2 February 1875.

136 Ibid., 905.

137 Ibid., 702.

138 Ibid., 1,742, 24 February 1874.

139 The rioting in Pittsburgh began on Saturday 21 July 1877 and the city was in full flame on Sunday. On Monday a meeting of citizens at the Chamber of Commerce called upon General Negley for his cooperation, *Pittsburgh Commercial Gazette*, 21 July 1877. A motion by Mr. Littell in the City Council put him in control of the armories in the city. See *The Daily Post*, 24 July 1877. According to these papers, he was active the remainder of the week. His Veteran Reserve Corps, numbering about six hundred was disbanded at the end of the week. James A. Henderson, "The Railroad Riots in Pittsburgh," *Western Pennsylvania Historical Magazine*, 11 (July 1928), 196.

140 These sketches are by no means independent of each other. A comparison of them is an interesting study in the demerits of some historiography.

141 In an obituary statement, *Pittsburgh Post*, 8 August 1901. The Pittsburgh and Western became a part of the B. & O. Railroad. It was earlier called the Pittsburgh, New Castle & Lake Erie Railroad. Family tradition states that General Negley lost much money in railroad building.

142 *Pittsburgh Directory for 1878 – 9*, 471. According to Henry V. Poor, *Manual of the Railroads of the United States for 1878 – 1879* (New York: H.V. & H.W. Poor, 1878), 377, J.S. Negley was a director. The same publication for 1879 lists him as "Vice-President." But he is not listed in the company in 1880. Reorganization followed a foreclosure sale.

143 *Pittsburgh Directory for 1882 – 83*, 568. Poor's *Manual of Railroads of the United States for 1884*, 354, mentions a new railroad, the New York, Pittsburgh and Chicago Railway of which James S. Negley was a director and "President" and J.S. Negley, Jr., Treasurer. General Negley held the same positions in 1885, but the railroad was absorbed by the Pittsburgh, Marion and Chicago in 1886, and General Negley no longer appears on its official list.

144 Consult the directories.

145 Consult the directories.

146 *Congressional Record*, 49th Cong., 1st Sess., 475, 6 January 1886.

147 Ibid., 2,742, 22 April 1886.

148 Ibid., 538, 7 January 1886.

149 Ibid., 2,379, 15 March 1886.

150 Ibid., 6,593.

151 Ibid., 5,830, 17 June 1886.

152 Ibid., 1,832 – 338, 26 February 1886.

153 Ibid., 3,705 – 6, 21 April 1886.

154 Ibid., 7,612 – 13.

155 Ibid., 1,458, 15 February 1886.

156 Ibid., 1,625, 18 February 1886.

157 Ibid., 731, 18 January 1886.

158 Ibid., 3,615 – 16, 9 April 1886.

159 Ibid., 731.

160 Ibid., 2nd Sess., 597, 12 January 1887; 1,172, 29 January 1887; 1,218, 31 January 1887.

161 Ibid., 269, 18 December 1886.

162 Ibid., 1,264.

163 Ibid., 1,822, 16 February 1887.

164 Ibid., 611.

165 Ibid., 792, 19 January 1887.

166 Ibid., 542, 11 January 1887.

167 I am informed by Mr. Robert Garland, who was present on the occasion that in his opinion this was the work of Christopher Magee. This information has been confirmed by others.

168 *Pittsburgh Daily Post*, 4 November 1886.

169 *Congressional Record*, passim. Also the testimony of Dr. William J. Holland of Pittsburgh.

170 His name ceased to appear in the *Directory* after the end of the directory year closing with 1 June 1887.

171 *Pittsburgh Post*, 8 August 1901.

172 Ibid.

173 *A Biographical Congressional Directory, 1774 – 1911*, 61st Cong. 2nd Sess., Senate Document No. 654, 887.

174 Statement of Dr. Holland.

175 *Pittsburgh Post*, 8 August 1901. Mr. James R. Mellon of Pittsburgh describes the relief on his tombstone as one of the finest sculptured likenesses he has ever seen.

176 Ibid.

177 Dr. William J. Holland, Mr. James R. Mellon, and Miss Georgina Negley, all of Pittsburgh.

178 *Year Book of the Pennsylvania Society of New York*, 75.

179 *History of Pittsburgh and Environs*, 4:62. According to the tombstone inscription, his son George G. Negley died 6 January 1870 and his son James S. Jr., died 21 February 1889.

180 Ibid.

CHAPTER 5
A BUCKTAIL VOICE: CIVIL WAR CORRESPONDENCE OF PRIVATE CORDELLO COLLINS

EDITED BY MARK REINSBERG

1 Pennsylvania governor Andrew Curtin equipped 13 regiments at state expense that became known as the Pennsylvania Reserve Regiments. Cordello Collin's regiment was the last raised, and was redesignated the 42nd Pennsylvania. Soldiers in the regiment affixed bucktails in their caps as a sign of marksmanship and distinction.

2 This became Company D in the formally organized regiment.

3 See U.S. Census of Warren County for years 1850 – 60.

4 Affidavits in the soldier's Pension file, especially that of Nathan Gibson and Albert Hartness of Warren County, 28 February 1881.

5 Possibly the engagement at Ball's Bluff, 21 October 1861.

6 Rasselas Brown, appointed president judge, Sixth Judicial District (Erie, Crawford and Warren counties) by Governor William Packer, 1860.

7 Cordello's eight brothers and sisters, in 1861, were: Amy, 16; Eveneaser, 15; John, 14; Morris, 13; Nancy, 11; DeWitt C., 10; Delilah, 7; and Prudence, 2.

8 O.R. Howard Thomson and William H. Rouch, *History of the Bucktails* (Philadelphia: Electric Prinbay Co., 1906), 11.

9 Lt. (later Capt.) John T.A. Jewett, who succeeded to command of Company D after the promotion of Roy Stone's successor, Hugh W. McNeil, to command of the Bucktail Regiment. Jewett had been a watchmaker in Warren prior to his enlistment in the Raftsmen's Guard.

10 Cordello's tentmate, and the relative of a near neighbor in Kinzua, Sylvester C. Hamlin, who had also enlisted in Roy Stone's original company.

11 Sylvester Hamlin was discharged on Surgeon's Certificate, 11 March 1862.

12 The motto "union forever" is penned over the calligraphy of his signature.

13 26 June near Atlee's Station. This skirmish was also known as Beaver Dam Creek.

14 Capt. Cooper's Battery B.

15 27 June at Gaines' Mill.

16 See Maj. Roy Stone's report of the Bucktail Regiment's participation in the Seven Days' Battles, in Official Records, series 1, volume 11, part 2, 400 – 19. Said General Truman Seymour, commanding the Third Division of which the Bucktails were a part, "Major Stone, with rare intelligence, prepared his position, and fought it like a true soldier to the end...." Cordello Collins was one of the 247 casualties, including missing, which reduced the regiment to 64 officers and enlisted men at the close of the campaign.

17 Arlington Heights, Virginia.

18 28 – 30 August, two days of fighting near Groveton, along the Warrenton Pike, culminating in the Second Battle of Bull Run. On 21 August the regiment marched from Falmouth, Virginia, in a heavy rainstorm, towards Kelley's Ford, twenty-seven miles away. It got lost on the road at night and halted to await daylight. On 22 August, the temperature reached 100 degrees, with "dust and mud lying inches thick." From Kelley's Ford, on the following day, the regiment marched to Rappahannock Station, bivouacking three miles from Warrenton. By 27 August, the Bucktails were in a position at Buckland Mills, near Gainsville.

19 Thomson and Rauch, *History of the Bucktails*, 179. "The First Brigade, under General Meade, seemed in one moment to reach the limits of its endurance. A murmur ran through its ranks and the column halted, ignoring its officers' orders to advance. General Meade rode back in person. Considerate as ever, he realized the calibre of the men with whom he had to deal. Briefly he told them that he recognized their sufferings; but explained that upon their reaching a certain point, on a certain day, depended the safety of a portion of General Pope's army and the lives of thousands of soldiers. Then he asked them what they wished to do; and ringing down the line came the answer: 'Go ahead.'"

20 Was this possible? I addressed an inquiry to Civil War historian Bruce Catton, who replied: "The soldier may have exaggerated the speed of the loading just a little, but I don't believe he was far off. A recent book on Civil War weapons remarks that the rate of fire of the Sharps was at least three times greater than the muzzle-loading Springfield. Since a good man could get at least two shots off a minute with the Springfield, this would bring the time required to load and fire the Sharps down to approximately ten seconds, and I have no doubt that once a veteran got used to the instrument, he could improve on that time materially." Personal correspondence, 17 November 1964.

21 Major General Irvin McDowell, then commanding the Third Corps.

22 The 1860 Census of Warren County, Pennsylvania, lists a John English family next following the Collins family. Susan was then 30 years old, one of three children living with the parents, in their late sixties. In *History of Warren County*, J.S. Schenck describes John English as "an honorable and successful farmer … also engaged to some extent in the lumber business." See J.S. Schenck, *History of Warren County* (Syracuse: D. Mason & Co., 1887), 478.

23 Near Sharpsburg, Maryland.

24 Sergeant Augustus A. Trask, of Youngsville, was killed at South Mountain, 14 September; Myron C. Cobb, of Spring Creek, fell at Antietam, 17 September; Henry H. Glazier also fell at Antietam; James Stewart, of Prince Edward Island, Canada, probably died a few days after the Battle of Antietam; but Nelson Geer, of Kinzua, survived his gunshot wound through the right lobe of the lungs, was given a medical discharge and lived until 1895. Glazier was not one of the original Raftsmen's Guard but a later recruit, presumably from Warren County.

25 William S. (J.?) Kibby (Kibbe or Kibbey, as the name variously appears) was one of Roy Stone's original followers, but he was transferred to Company I of the Bucktail Regiment, where he became a first Sgt. He was wounded at South Mountain, 14 September, and died 18 September. The earliest roll of the Raftsmen's Guard lists his residence at McKean County.

26 Col. Hugh W. McNeil, of Auburn, New York, originally, briefly of Warren, commanded the Bucktails from January 1862. He was 1st Lt. in Captain Stone's original Company D, becoming captain of that company when a vacancy occurred, without opposition from Major Stone. Two months before Antietam, Stone had been released by the regiment to recruit a new Bucktail brigade, which was in training in the Washington area as these events took place. McNeil had been a bank cashier in Warren, Pennsylvania, at the start of the war. He was killed while leading a charge, 16 September, during skirmishing prior to the Battle of Antietam.

27 Captains McDonald, of Company G, and McGee, of Company F. Several had been wounded or captured in previous engagements, and had not yet returned. Two had been wounded in this engagement. One had been killed in an earlier battle, and another had resigned to accept command of a newly-formed regiment, and neither of these vacancies had been filled prior to South Mountain.

28 The 1860 U.S. Census of Warren Company lists Loren Labree, 19, as a member of the Smith Labree family in Kinzua. According to Schenck's history of that county, Cordello Collins' friend Loren "served

under Captain D.W.C. James, of Warren, in the last company of volunteer infantry raised in the State, and was also in the last volunteer battery raised in the State under Captain William Barrows."

29 John Collins had purchased about 50 acres of land from Robert Campbell early in the war years. Cordello's bounty money, about $200, was used as the down payment, plus monthly installments of his soldier's pay. (Affidavit signed by Robert Campbell dated 3 March 1882, at Kane, Pennsylvania) In the 1860 Census, Campbell was 52, a farmer in Kinzua, five children still at home.

30 Orris Hall, 1804 – 81, a merchant of Warren, with lumber, oil, and real estate interests – one of the substantial men of the county. He was father of two boys in the regiment, one of whom, Sgt. Roscoe Hall, had already been killed at Second Bull Run. His nephew, the Lt. Robert Hall referred to in the first paragraph of this letter, was killed at Gettysburg.

31 The famous "Mud March," an abortive flank attack conceived by Major General Ambrose Everett Burnside, commanding the Army of the Potomac, 7 November 1862 – 27 January 1863.

32 Near Washington, D.C.

CHAPTER 6
SOME ASPECTS OF PITTSBURGH'S INDUSTRIAL CONTRIBUTIONS TO THE CIVIL WAR

BY LOUIS VAIRA

1   *Pittsburgh Dispatch*, 25 December 1860.
2   Erasmus Wilson, *Standard History of Pittsburgh, Pennsylvania* (Chicago: H.R. Cornell & Campus, 1898), 548.
3   Ibid.
4   *Pittsburgh Dispatch*, 23 December 1860.
5   *Pittsburgh Gazette*, 4 January 1861.
6   Warren D. Crandall, *History of the Ram Fleet and The Mississippi Marine Brigade in the War for the Union on the Mississippi and its Territories* (St. Louis: Press of Buschart Brothers, 1907), 19.
7   Ibid., 27.
8   Ibid., 28.
9   Ibid., 17.
10 Ibid., *passim*.
11 *American Annual Cyclopedia*, I (1861), 504.
12 *American Annual Cyclopedia*, II (1862), 607.
13 Frank M. Bennett, *Steam Navy of the United States* (Pittsburgh: Warren & Company, 1898), Appendix B.
14 *Gazette*, 10 February 1862.
15 George H. Thurston, *Pittsburgh and Allegheny in the Centennial Year* (Pittsburgh: A.A. Anderson & Son, 1876), 100ff.
16 Bennett, *Steam Navy of the United States*, Appendix B.
17 Thurston, *Pittsburgh and Allegheny in the Centennial Year*, 102.
18 Bennett, *Steam Navy of the United States*, Appendix B.
19 *Gazette*, 10 February 1862.
20 Bennett, *Steam Navy of the United States*, Appendix B.
21 H.K. White, letter to author.
22 *Gazette*, 5 May 1862.
23 Ibid., 5 December 1861.
24 Leonder S. Bishop, *History of American Manufacturers, from 1608 to 1860* (Philadelphia: Edward Young and Company, 1864), 2:581.
25 Thurston, *Pittsburgh and Allegheny in the Centennial Year*, 171.
26 *Pittsburgh Evening Chronicle*, 3 June 1861.
27 *Gazette*, 30 August 1861.
28 *Pittsburgh Evening Chronicle*, 5 June 1862.

29 *House Exec. Docs.*, 40 Cong., 2 Sess., No. 99, 805 – 16.

30 *House Exec. Docs.*, 38 Cong., 1 Sess., No. 1, 106; 38 Cong., 2 Sess., No. 83, 117; 38 Cong., 1 Sess., No. 1, 998.

31 Ibid., 40 Cong., 2 Sess., No. 99, 698 – 996.

32 *Gazette*, 29 September 1862.

33 *House Exec. Docs.*, 38 Cong., 2 Sess., No. 1., 975.

34 *Gazette*, 29 September 1861.

35 *House Exec. Docs.*, 40 Cong., 2 Sess., No. 99., 813.

36 *Gazette*, 29 September 1861.

37 United States Congress, Joint Committee on the Conduct on the War, *Report of the Joint Committee on the Conduct of War* (Washington, D.C.: Government Publication Office, 1861), 2:87.

38 *House Exec. Docs.*, 40 Cong., 2 Sess., No. 99., 805.

39 Ibid., 40 Cong., 2 Sess., No. 99., 225.

40 Ibid., 40 Cong., 2 Sess., No. 99., 720; 805 – 11; 815f; 724; 976f.

41 Ibid., 38 Cong., 1 Sess., No., 106.

42 Ibid., 40 Cong., 2 Sess., No. 99., 977f; 811 – 17.

43 Ibid., 38 Cong., 3 Sess., No. 83. 698 – 996.

44 *Official Records of the War of the Rebellion* (Washington, D.C.: Government Printing Office, 1880), series 3, vol. 2, 811.

45 W.A. Lare and W.M. Hartzell, *Rebellion Record of Allegheny County* (Pittsburgh: A.A. Anderson, 1862), 45f.

46 *Official Records of the War of the Rebellion*, series 3, vol. 2, 811.

47 Thurston, *Pittsburgh and Allegheny in the Centennial Year*, 145.

CHAPTER 7
THE SANITARY FAIR

BY DOROTHY DANIEL

1   United States Archives. [The endnotes for this article are noticeably incomplete. In footnotes one and two, the author did not specify which collections she used, citing only the United States Archives as the source. Similarly, in note six, she merely mentions the archives of the Historical Society of Western Pennsylvania, not the specific archival collections that were examined.]

2   United States Archives.

3   James Veech papers, Historical Society of Western Pennsylvania.

4   Ibid.

5   Ibid.

6   Archives, Historical Society of Western Pennsylvania

7   *Pittsburgh Post*, 30 May 1864

8   *Pittsburgh Gazette*, 1 June 1864

9   *Pittsburgh Post*, 2 June 1864

10 Ibid., 3 June 1864

11 Ibid., 3 June 1864

12 James Veech papers, Historical Society of Western Pennsylvania.
    General Sources: United States Archives; Files of the *Pittsburgh Post Gazette*, May – June 1864; Files of the *Daily Post*, May–June 1864; Records of the United States Sanitary Commission.

CHAPTER 8
THE PITTSBURGH SOLDIERS' AND SAILORS' CONVENTION, 25-26 SEPTEMBER 1866

BY CHARLES D. CASHDOLLAR

1   Claude Bowers, *The Tragic Era* (Cambridge: Houghton Mifflin Company, 1929), 138.
2   *Pittsburgh Gazette*, 26 September 1866, hereinafter cited as Gazette.
3   James Blaine, *Twenty Years of Congress* (Norwich, Conn.: The Henry Hill Publishing Company, 1886), II:232 – 33.
4   Eric McKitrick, *Andrew Johnson and Reconstruction* (Chicago: The University of Chicago Press, 1960), 258.
5   Ibid., 274.
6   James F. Rhodes, *History of the United States* (New York: The Macmillan Company, 1928), VI:96. The three were Postmaster General William Dennison, Attorney-General James Speed, and Secretary of the Interior James Harlan.
7   Blaine, *Twenty Years of Congress*, II:220.
8   Howard K. Beale, *The Critical Year* (New York: Frederick Ungar Publishing Co., 1958), 131 – 33.
9   Ibid., 131; Bowers, *The Tragic Era*, 124.
10 Blaine, *Twenty Years of Congress*, II:221 – 23.
11 Ibid., 221. Bowers states that Johnson's own Secretary of War, E.M. Stanton, was instrumental in the organization of this rival convention. See Bowers, *The Tragic Era*, 125.
12 Bowers, *The Tragic Era*, 125.
13 Beale, *The Critical Year*, 331, quoting the *New York Herald*, 6 September 1866.
14 Blaine, *Twenty Years of Congress*, II:226.
15 Ibid., II:226.
16 John W. Burgess, *Reconstruction and the Constitution* (New York: Charles Scribner's Sons, 1902), 101.
17 Blaine, *Twenty Years of Congress*, II:228 – 29.
18 *Gazette*, 22 September 1866.
19 Ibid., 25 and 26 September 1866.
20 Blaine, *Twenty Years of Congress*, II:230.
21 *Gazette*, 25 September 1866. General Grant still remaining aloof from the Radical cause did not attend the convention. The *Pittsburgh Post* records that he spent the afternoon of 25 September 1866, in Jerome Park, New York, watching Bag Water win the mile and a quarter dash. See *Pittsburgh Post*, 26 September 1866.
22 *Gazette*, 27 September 1866.
23 Ibid., 25 September 1866.
24 Ibid.
25 Ibid. The Wigwam was 120 feet wide and 200 feet long. The roof of the structure collapsed on Sunday afternoon, 23 September, injuring some Sunday afternoon strollers who were inspecting the shelter. It was repaired and strengthened on Monday before inspectors judged it safe for use by the convention. See *Gazette*, 24 September 1866.
26 *Gazette*, 26 September 1866.
27 *Pittsburgh Post*, 27 September 1866, hereinafter cited as *Post*. In the fall elections, Geary defeated Clymer by a majority of 17,176. He served for two terms, being reelected in 1869 by a majority of 4,000. Wayland Dunaway, *A History of Pennsylvania* (New York: Prentice-Hall, 1946), 527.
29 *Post*, 27 September 1866.
30 *Gazette*, 25 September 1866.
31 Ibid., 27 September 1866.
32 Ibid., 26 September 1866.
33 Ibid.
34 Ibid., 25 September 1866.
35 Ibid., 25 and 26 September 1866.

36   Ibid., 29 September 1866.
37   *New York Times*, 26 September 1866.
38   *Post*, 26 September 1866.
39   *Gazette*, 26 September 1866.
40   Ibid.
41   *Post*, 27 September 1866. "Jayhawk" in Kansas parlance is synonymous with "lynch."
42   *Gazette*, 27 September 1866.
43   Ibid.
44   *Gazette*, 28 September 1866.
45   *Post*, 27 September 1866.
46   Ibid., 28 September 1866.
47   Ibid.
48   *Gazette*, 27 September 1866. This is the same Butler who was accused of stealing silver spoons during his occupation of New Orleans. The Democrats accused the Radicals of urging Butler to come to Pittsburgh by saying that the houses of the citizens would be thrown open in welcome. They seriously doubted that he would find much silver in Pittsburgh. The *Post* ran a small poem expressing its feelings toward the Radical hero: "Ben Butler was a soldier brave/ a soldier brave was he,/ He had for silver spoons and sich,/ A par-ti-ali-t-y." [sic]
49   Ibid.
50   Ibid.
51   Ibid.
52   Ibid.
53   Ibid.
54   Ibid.
55   Ibid.
56   *Gazette*, 25 September 1866.
57   As quoted by the *Gazette*, 27 September 1866.
58   *New York Times*, 26 and 27 September 1866.
59   *New York Times*, 27 September 1866.
60   Blaine, *Twenty Years of Congress*, II:233.
61   *Gazette*, 27 September 1866.
62   Blaine, *Twenty Years of Congress*, II:233.
63   *Gazette*, 25 September 1866.
64   Blaine, *Twenty Years of Congress*, II:233.
65   William Dunning, *Reconstruction: Political and Economic* (New York: Harper, 1907), 78.

APPENDIX

This list, courtesy of the HSWP Library & Archives, gathers more than 60 Civil War articles that have appeared in *Western Pennsylvania Historical Magazine, Pittsburgh History,* and *Western Pennsylvania History,* grouped by subject. It has been adapted and updated for this book. The eight articles that appear in this volume are marked with a star.

Campaigns/Battles
"The Confederate Raid at Morgantown, West Virginia"
Edited by Myron B. Sharp
Vol. 50 (Oct. 1967), p. 335
    Included are selections from the Mathiot Papers, held at the Historical Society of Western Pennsylvania, detailing the raid of April 27, 1863.

Regimental and Other Unit Histories
"Pittsburgh Volunteers with Sickles' Excelsior Brigade" (in four parts)
By Bruce Sutherland
Vol. 45 (March, June, Sept., Dec. 1962), pps. 47, 147, 241, 309
    Narrative of the brigade's operations throughout the war. The brigade was composed of New York regiments, but included in the 70th the Pittsburgh Friend Rifles as Company E and the Pittsburgh Zouave Cadets as Company A in the 74th. Another Western Pennsylvania company (from Tidioute, Warren County) formed part of Companies F and H of the 74th.

"Colonel Samuel M. Jackson and the Eleventh Pennsylvania Reserves"
By Frank W. Jackson
Vol. 18 (March 1935), p. 45
    In May 1861, the Pennsylvania General Assembly created the Pennsylvania Reserve Corps, consisting of 13 infantry, one cavalry, and one light artillery regiment. The corps was mustered into U.S. service in June 1861 and mustered out in June 1864, and was commanded at various times by Generals McCall, Reynolds, Meade, and Crawford. Sustaining the most casualties of the corps in 16 battles was the Eleventh, recruited in Western Pennsylvania and commanded by Col. Samuel M. Jackson.

"Descent of the Raftsmen's Guard: A Roll Call"
By Mark Reinsberg
Vol. 53 (Jan. 1970), p. 1
    Biographical sketches of the men of the Warren County company that became Company D of the 13th Pennsylvania Reserves (Bucktail Regiment).

"A Brief History of Company A, 139th Regiment, Pennsylvania Volunteers"
By Edward M. McConnell
Vol. 55 (Oct. 1972), p. 308
    Company A was recruited in Mercer County in August 1862. Based in part on the papers of Capt. Abraham H. Snyder and Pvt. Jonathan E. Beil, both killed at the Battle of the Wilderness.

Biography/Autobiography

"Discipline and Piety: Professor, General, and College President John Fraser"
By Jim Weeks
Vol. 76 (Spring 1993), p. 24

A short biography of Fraser, a professor at Jefferson College, who was appointed Colonel and c‑mander of the 140th Regiment, Pennsylvania Volunteer Infantry, and later a Brigade commander. He participated in the Battles of Chancellorville, Gettysburg, the Wilderness, Spotsylvania, and Petersbur‑ where he was captured and spent months in Confederate prisons. After the war, he served as president of Penn State and Kansas Universities, both unsuccessfully, and finished his career as a professor at the University of Pittsburgh.

"Matthew Stanley Quay"
By John W. Oliver
Vol. 17 (March 1934), p. 1

Quay was a Beaver County politician and local leader of the Republican Party. He was elected to the Pennsylvania General Assembly and U.S. Senate following the Civil War. During the War, among other appointments, he was Colonel and commander of the 134th Regiment, Pennsylvania Volunteer Infantry, and won the Congressional Medal of Honor for valor at Fredericksburg.

"The Exploration of a Legend"
By Frank Pollicino
Vol. 53 (July 1970), p. 243

Short biography of Harry White, an Indiana County politician who was appointed Major of the 67th Regiment, Pennsylvania Volunteer Infantry, served during the War, was a prisoner of war until exchanged in 1864 and was mustered out as a Brigadier General.

★ "General James Scott Negley"
By Alfred P. James
Vol. 14 (Apr. 1931), p. 69

Negley, a Pittsburgher, rose to the rank of Major General in charge of a Division, mostly operating in the Western Theater. He was later a long-time U.S. Congressman.

"The Pittsburgh Rifles and the Battle of Drainesville: Alexander Murdoch"
Edited by Robert A. Jones
Vol. 53 (July 1970), p. 299

Short biography of Alexander Murdoch, who enlisted for three years in the Pittsburgh Rifles, Company A, 9th Pennsylvania Reserves, 38th Regiment, Pennsylvania Volunteer Infantry. Also includes Murdoch's speech in honor of his unit's reunion on December 19, 1885.

Diaries/Personal Narratives/Letters

"Some Leaves from a Civil War Diary"
Edited by Harry R. Beck
Vol. 42 (Dec. 1959), p. 363

Excerpts from the diary of Corp. Florence C. Biggert, covering his active duty on three separate occasions: as a member of the 15th Regiment of Pennsylvania Militia in September 1862, serving as reserves at the Battle of Antietem and in June 1863 as guards for the City of Pittsburgh just prior to the Battle of Gettysburg, and as a member of Capt. Knap's artillery battery during July – August 1863 guarding communication lines following Gettysburg. After the war, Biggert entered the insurance business.

ncis Marion Elliott, A Pennsylvania Country Boy"

d reaction to the war.

Arthurs"

scribes how, to find his brother, he posed as an Army surgeon for two months.

Craig's Memoirs of Civil War and Reconstruction" (in five parts)
uscript of memoirs furnished by his son Mark R. Craig.
930), p. 215; Vol. 14 (Jan., Apr., July, Oct. 1931), pps. 43, 115, 191, 258
was a Captain and commander of Company B, 105th Regiment, Pennsylvania Volunteer Infantry,
npany A, 17th Regiment, Veteran Reserve Corps.

"A Bucktail Voice: Civil War Correspondence of Private Cordello Collins"
Edited by Mark Reinsberg
Vol. 48 (July 1965), p. 235

From Warren County, Collins enlisted in the Raftsmen's Guard, Company D of the Bucktails, 42nd Regiment, Pennsylvania Volunteer Infantry. He died of wounds at the Battle of Gettysburg in August 1863. The letters are addressed primarily to his parents.

"A Confederate Girl Visits Pennsylvania, July – September 1863" (in two parts)
Edited by Ernest M. Lander
Vol. 49 (Apr. 1966), p. 111; (July 1966), p. 197

The article includes correspondence from Floride Clemson to her mother during a trip to visit relatives in Pennsylvania in 1863. Her father and brother had left the family home in Maryland to aid the Southern cause.

"Civil War Diary of an Ohio Volunteer"
Edited by Donald J. Coan
Vol. 50 (July 1967), p. 171

The author, William Thompson Daugherty, was a member of Company B, 104th Ohio Volunteer Infantry. He was from Greentown, Ohio. The diary covers the period from January 1, 1864 to December 31, 1864, shortly after the Battle of Franklin, Tenn.

"The Civil War Letters of James Rush Holmes"
Edited by Ida Bright Adams
Vol. 44 (June 1961), p. 105

The 1861 – 65 letters from Holmes, a sergeant with the 61st Regiment, Pennsylvania Volunteer Infantry, focuses primarily on camp life.

"Dear Sister Jennie – Dear Brother Jacob: The Correspondence Between a Northern Soldier and His Sister in Mechanicsburg, Pennsylvania, 1861 – 1864" (in two parts)
Edited by Florence C. McLaughlin
Vol. 60 (Apr. 1977), p. 109; (July 1977), p. 203

Jacob Heffelfinger, the soldier, was a member of the Seventh Regiment, Pennsylvania Reserves.

"The Confederate Memorial at West Park in Pittsburgh"
By Gregg L. Neel
Vol. 20 (Sept. 1937), p. 215
    Dedication of a memorial tablet at the site of the old Western Penitentiary, which served as t
in 1863 – 64 for 118 junior officers and enlisted men of Maj. General John H. Morgan's Confederate
after his surrender in June 1863.

"Diary of Salisbury Prison"
By James W. Eberhart. Edited by Florence C. McLaughlin.
Vol. 56 (July 1973), p. 211
    Eberhart was a sergeant in Company G, 8th Pennsylvania Reserve Volunteer Corps, and Company G,
191st Pennsylvania Veteran Volunteers. He was imprisoned at Belle Isle and Salisbury Prisons from August
19, 1864, when he was captured at Petersburg, until February 22, 1865, when he was paroled. See also the
footnote in Vol. 57 (Jan. 1974), p. 127, concerning the dedication in 1910 of the Pennsylvania monument at
Salisbury Cemetery.

Political Affairs
"Abraham Lincoln in Pittsburgh and the Birth of the Republican Party"
By Charles W. Dahlinger
Vol. 3 (Oct. 1920), p. 145
    The article is followed by a tribute to Abraham Lincoln, with no author listed.

★ "Western Pennsylvania and the Election of 1860"
By Joseph P. Wolstoncraft
Vol. 6 (Jan. 1923), p. 25

"The Election of 1864 in Western Pennsylvania"
By Norman C. Brillhart
Vol. 8 (Jan. 1925), p. 26

"Senator Edgar A. Cowan, 1861 – 1867"
By B.F. Pershing
Vol. 4 (Oct. 1921), p. 224
    Political career of a U.S. Senator during the Civil War.

"Honest John Covode"
By A. John Dodds
Vol. 15 (Aug. 1933), p. 175
    Covode was a Westmoreland politician who was a member of Congress during the first few years of
the Civil War and, at the time, was Chairman of the Joint Committee on the Conduct of the War. Reelected
in 1866, he opposed President Johnson's reconstruction policies.

"The Civil War Career of Andrew Gregg Curtin, Governor of Pennsylvania" (in three parts)
By Rebecca Gifford Albright
Vol. 47 (Oct. 1964), p. 323; Vol. 48 (Jan. and Apr. 1965), pps. 19 and 151
    A detailed look at Curtin's career as a moderate war governor, a strong supporter of Lincoln's
administration.

"Jeremiah Sullivan Black and the Great Secession Winter"
By John T. Hubbell
Vol. 57 (July 1974), p. 255
    Black's role as Attorney General in President Buchanan's cabinet on the eve of the Civil War.

"Pennsylvania Senate Deadlock"

...ajor Harry White became a prisoner of war in Libby Prison.

..ers in Pennsylvania in 1861"

...a response to the shipment of illegal goods to the South, suspected spys, and
..ers in Pennsylvania in 1861.

..ty/City Histories
..g Pittsburgh in 1863"
..nn P. Cowan
..l. 2 (Jan. 1919), p. 59
A historic document gives an interesting record of the men who worked on the construction of Coal Hill Fort.

"Pittsburgh's Civil War Fortification Claims"
By Henry King Siebeneck
Vol. 27 (March – June 1944), p. 1
Discusses the fortification of Pittsburgh by Maj. General William T.H. Brooks, Department of the Monongahela, through the efforts of numerous private industrial and commercial firms during Lee's 1863 invasion of Pennsylvania and the denial of most of the claims for compensation following the war.

"Thirty Days of Panic"
By George Swetnam
Vol. 51 (Oct. 1968), p. 329
Story of the fortification of Pittsburgh in the weeks before the Battle of Gettysburg.

★ "Some Aspects of Pittsburgh's Industrial Contributions to the Civil War"
By Louis Vaira
Vol. 6 (Jan. 1923), p. 9

"Pittsburgh's Negro Troops in the Civil War"
By George L. Davis
Vol. 36 (June 1953), p. 101

"A Lost Landmark: A Study of the Fate of the Allegheny Arsenal"
By James Wudarczyk
Vol. 70 (Apr. 1987), p. 191

★ "New Castle in 1860 – 61: A Community Response to a War Crisis"
By Bingham Duncan
Vol. 24 (Dec. 1941), p. 251
Describes pre-Sumter attitudes toward the South and war efforts immediately after the beginning of the war.

"Pennsylvania Raises an Army, 1861"
By Dr. Edward G. Everett
Vol. 39 (Summer 1956), p. 83
Focuses on the raising of the initial Pennsylvania three-month regiments in April 1861.

"One Month in the Summer of '63: Pittsburgh Prepares for the Civil War" (in two parts)
By Bill McCarthy
Vol. 81 (Fall and Winter 1998), pps. 118, 156
    The second part includes a detailed list of the various fortifications.

"Carnegie's Civil War Time Capsule"
By Jessica Ream and Brian Butko
Vol. 81 (Winter 1998), p. 170
    Recalls the Captain Thomas Espy Post of the GAR in Carnegie, Pa., its closing in 1937, and the artifac
found missing when it was reopened in 1984.

Miscellaneous
"Writing History from Civil War Newspapers"
By J. Cutler Andrews
Vol. 54 (Jan. 1971), p. 1
    Anecdotes involving Civil War newspaper correspondents.

"The Buried "Broken-Back Ducks" 200,000 Fifty-Cent Pieces: What would they be worth today"
By Ardis Jones Blenko
Vol. 59 (Jan. 1976), p. 84
    The burial by the Economites of $100,000 in coin at the time of General Morgan's cavalry raid in
eastern Ohio, 1863.

★ "The Pittsburgh Soldiers' and Sailors' Convention, September 25 – 26, 1866"
By Charles D. Cashdollar
Vol. 48 (Oct. 1965), p. 331
    An anti-President Johnson national convention of veterans of the Civil War, supporting a harsh
reconstruction.

"Pennsylvania Newspapers and Public Opinion, 1861 – 1862"
By Edward G. Everett
Vol. 44 (March 1961), p. 1
    Analyzes the state's newspapers and their attacks on opponents of the war and the Republican
administration.

"Andrew Carnegie's Civil War Profits"
By Edwin S. Fickes
Vol. 17 (March 1934), p. 77
    The article concludes that Carnegie's interests in iron manufacture were too late to have participated
in Civil War defense contracts.

"An Annotated Bibliography of Civil War-Era Articles in Pennsylvania Journals, 1893 – 1982"
Compiled and edited by John Kent Folmar.
Vol. 66 (July 1983), p. 293
    This list includes 139 major articles, some with brief descriptions, from 868 issues of three journals:
The Pennsylvania Magazine of History and Biography; Pennsylvania History; and *Western Pennsylvania
Historical Magazine.*

"The Pittsburgh Sanitary Fair"
By Charles W. Dahlinger
Vol. 12 (Apr. 1929), p. 97

ABRIDGED INDEX